교과서 필수 문법으로 익히는 영어 문장 쓰기

WRITING BUILDER

1

WRITING BUILDER 1

지은이	NE능률 영어교육연구소
선임연구원	김동숙
연구원	양빈나 강혜진 이지연 최효정
영문 교열	Patrick Ferraro, Amanda Brockus, Daniel Baum
디자인	윤혜정 윤성준 김지연
내지 일러스트	끌레몽 윤예지
표지 일러스트	김나영
맥편집	김재민

Let's grow together

NE능률이
미래를
창조합니다.

건강한 배움의 고객가치를 제공하겠다는 꿈을 실현하기 위해
40년이 넘는 시간 동안 열심히 달려왔습니다.

앞으로도 끊임없는 연구와 노력을 통해
당연한 것을 멈추지 않고

고객, 기업, 직원 모두가 함께 성장하는 NE능률이 되겠습니다.

서문

최근 우리나라 영어 교육의 가장 큰 특징은 실용 영어의 중시와 함께
말하기, 쓰기와 같은 표현 영어를 강조하는 방향으로 변화하고 있다는
점입니다. 근래에 들어 말하기, 쓰기 능력을 평가하려는 시도가
활발해지고 있는 것도 이러한 변화의 일환입니다. 특히 쓰기는 인터넷과
이메일 등 글을 통한 세계와의 접촉이 활발해지는 상황에서 자기 생각을
정확하게 표현하기 위해 반드시 길러야 하는 능력입니다.

쓰기 실력을 향상시키기 위해서는 논리력, 구성력, 표현력 등 여러 가지
능력을 연마해야 합니다. 하지만 우선 영어 문장을 제대로 쓰기 위해
문장의 구조 및 영문법을 이해한 후 이를 바탕으로 충분히 연습해야
합니다. 이에 Writing Builder는 자주 쓰는 문형 및 문법을 익혀 이를
토대로 문장을 써보는 단계적인 학습을 통해 쓰기의 기본기를 탄탄히
쌓을 수 있도록 구성하였습니다. 또한 실생활과 밀접한 상황과 실용문을
통해 영어 문장 쓰기에 친근하게 접근할 수 있도록 하고 풍부한 연습
문제로 영작에 익숙해질 수 있도록 하였습니다.

Writing Builder를 통해 여러분은 영어 문장 쓰는 것에 자신감을
갖고, 나아가 자기 생각을 글로 표현할 수 있게 될 것입니다. Writing
Builder가 영어로 글쓰기의 기본을 쌓고자 할 때는 물론, 쓰기 서술형
평가를 준비할 때에도 소중한 디딤돌이 되었으면 합니다.

목차

구성과 특징

영어 문장 쓰기 핵심 Point 정리
문장 쓰기의 기본을 다지는 데 필요한 영어 문장 구조와 문법 사항을 간단명료하게
설명했습니다. 실용적인 예문을 제시하여 한 눈에 보기 쉽게 정리하였습니다.

추가 문법 사항 정리
핵심 Point와 함께 알아 두면 좋은 문법 사항을
정리해 두었습니다.

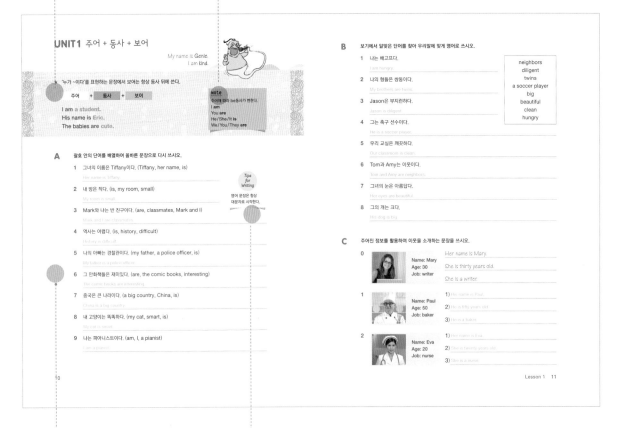

영어 문장 쓰기의 기본기 다지기
영어 문장 쓰기 실력을 향상시키는 데 필요한 기본적인
기술을 간략하게 설명하였습니다. 이를 통해 좀 더 정확한
문장을 쓸 수 있도록 하였습니다.

다양한 문제 유형을 통한 핵심 Point 연습
다양한 형태의 쓰기 문제를 통해 앞서 학습한 문장 구조 및 문법 사항의 이해도를
점검하고 문장 쓰기의 기초를 마련할 수 있도록 하였습니다.

연습 문제로 핵심 사항 정리

다양하고 심화된 연습 문제로 앞서 학습한 언어 표현과 쓰기 기술을 복습하고, 문장 쓰기에 익숙해질 수 있도록 하였습니다.

영어로 우리말 표현하기

완전한 문장을 직접 써 봄으로써 우리말을 영어로 표현하는 데 자신감을 키울 수 있도록 하였습니다.

실용문과 서술형 평가 문제로 응용력 기르기

앞서 학습한 표현을 활용하여 일기, 이메일, 광고문 등의 실용문을 완성해 보고, 서술형 평가와 유사한 문제를 풀어봄으로써 응용력을 기를 수 있도록 하였습니다.

필수 문장 표현 익히기

사용 빈도가 높은 문장 패턴을 선별하여
실생활에서 자주 쓰이는 문장 표현에 익숙해질 수
있도록 하였습니다.

어휘 복습하기

Lesson별 중요 어휘를 복습하고 암기할 수
있도록 하였습니다.

Useful Patterns for Writing 1

* one's favorite ~ is …: ~가 가장 좋아하는 ~는 …이다
My favorite sport **is** soccer.

* hate + 목적어: ~을 싫어한다
I hate summer.

1 내가 가장 좋아하는 색은 파란색이다.

2 Alex는 테니스를 싫어한다.

3 Kate가 가장 좋아하는 음식은 피자다.

4 내 남동생은 뜨거운 우유를 싫어한다.

5 Anne이 가장 좋아하는 도시는 로마이다. (Rome)

6 그는 수학을 싫어한다. (math)

7 Nick이 가장 좋아하는 과목은 영어다.

8 Emma는 공포영화를 싫어한다. (horror movies)

9 그녀가 가장 좋아하는 달은 4월이다.

10 나는 월요일 아침을 싫어한다.

LESSON 1

student 학생	treat 치료하다
cute 귀여운	sick 아픈
classmate 반 친구	cook 요리사, 요리하다
history 역사	delicious 맛있는
difficult 어려운	sportsman 운동선수
police officer 경찰관	actress 여배우
comic book 만화책	science 과학
country 나라	class 수업
smart 똑똑한	scary 무서운
pianist 피아니스트	friendly 다정한
hungry 배고픈	clothes 옷
twin 쌍둥이	wear 쓰고 있다
diligent 부지런한	same 같은
player 선수	similar 비슷한
classroom 교실	glasses 안경
neighbor 이웃	place 장소
beautiful 아름다운	visit 방문하다
writer 작가	service 서비스
baker 제빵사	fast 빠른
nurse 간호사	sushi 초밥
magic 마법의	fresh 신선한
power 힘	slow 느린
ride 타다	
bike 자전거	
bake (음식을) 굽다	### LESSON 2
magazine 잡지	
teach 가르치다	neckache 목의 통증
math 수학	secret 비밀
drama 드라마	funny 우스운
learn 배우다	joke 농담
yoga 요가	parent 부모
collect 수집하다	question 질문
school uniform 교복	clock 시계
check 확인하다	eraser 지우개
download 다운로드 하다	lend 빌려주다
rabbit 토끼	gift 선물
hamster 햄스터	bring 가져오다
vegetable 야채	story 이야기
meat 고기	dinner 저녁
thin 마른	science 과학
businessman 회사원	homework 숙제
heavy 무거운	handsome 잘생긴
famous 유명한	skin 피부
slim 날씬한	special 특별한
basketball 농구	lie 거짓말
elementary school 초등학교	keep 유지하다
short 키가 작은	angry 화난
	novel 소설
	genius 천재

SECTION 1
SENTENCE STRUCTURE

LESSON 1

문장의 형식 Ⅰ

classmate	beautiful	vegetable	sportsman
history	writer	meat	actress
police officer	baker	thin	scary
country	ride	businessman	friendly
smart	bake	heavy	clothes
hungry	magazine	famous	similar
twin	math	slim	glasses
diligent	collect	treat	visit
classroom	school uniform	cook	fast
neighbor	check	delicious	fresh

UNIT1 주어 + 동사 + 보어

My name is Genie.
I am kind.

★ '누가 ~이다'를 표현하는 문장에서 보어는 항상 동사 뒤에 쓴다.

주어	+	동사	+	보어

I **am** a student.
His name **is** Eric.
The babies **are** cute.

A 괄호 안의 단어를 배열하여 올바른 문장으로 다시 쓰시오.

1 그녀의 이름은 Tiffany이다. (Tiffany, her name, is)

_____

2 내 방은 작다. (is, my room, small)

_____

3 Mark와 나는 반 친구이다. (are, classmates, Mark and I)

_____

4 역사는 어렵다. (is, history, difficult)

_____

5 나의 아빠는 경찰관이다. (my father, a police officer, is)

_____

6 그 만화책들은 재미있다. (are, the comic books, interesting)

_____

7 중국은 큰 나라이다. (a big country, China, is)

_____

8 내 고양이는 똑똑하다. (my cat, smart, is)

_____

9 나는 피아니스트이다. (am, I, a pianist)

_____

Tips for Writing

영어 문장은 항상
대문자로 시작한다.

B 보기에서 알맞은 단어를 찾아 우리말에 맞게 영어로 쓰시오.

1 나는 배고프다.

2 나의 형들은 쌍둥이다.

3 Jason은 부지런하다.

4 그는 축구 선수이다.

5 우리 교실은 깨끗하다.

6 Tom과 Amy는 이웃이다.

7 그녀의 눈은 아름답다.

8 그의 개는 크다.

neighbors
diligent
twins
a soccer player
big
beautiful
clean
hungry

C 주어진 정보를 활용하여 이웃을 소개하는 문장을 쓰시오.

0 Name: Mary
Age: 30
Job: writer

Her name is Mary.
She is thirty years old.
She is a writer.

1 Name: Paul
Age: 50
Job: baker

1)
2)
3)

2  Name: Eva
Age: 20
Job: nurse

1)
2)
3)

UNIT 2 주어 + 동사 + 목적어

I have **magic powers.**
You need **me.**

★ '~을 …하다'를 표현하는 문장에서 목적어는 항상 동사 뒤에 쓴다.

| 주어 | + | 동사 | + | 목적어 |

I **have** many friends.
Bill **knows** my phone number.
His friends **like** online games.

A 괄호 안의 단어를 배열하여 올바른 문장으로 다시 쓰시오.

1 나는 자전거를 탄다. (I, a bike, ride)

_____

2 Travis는 빵을 굽는다. (Travis, bread, bakes)

_____

3 나는 베이컨 샌드위치를 원한다. (want, I, a bacon sandwich)

_____

4 Nick은 치즈 케이크를 싫어한다. (Nick, cheesecake, hates)

_____

5 Eddy는 많은 야구 모자를 가지고 있다. (many baseball caps, has, Eddy)

_____

6 Susan은 패션 잡지를 읽는다. (Susan, a fashion magazine, reads)

_____

7 나의 아빠는 수학을 가르치신다. (teaches, math, my father)

_____

8 Stella는 긴 머리를 가지고 있다. (long hair, Stella, has)

_____

9 수정이와 민수는 미국 드라마를 좋아한다.
   (like, American dramas, Sujeong and Minsu)

_____

Tips for Writing

평서문 끝에는 항상
마침표(.)를 찍는다.

B 각 보기에서 알맞은 표현을 찾아 우리말에 맞게 영어로 쓰시오.

| read |
| know |
| check |
| collect |
| learn |
| wear |
| love |
| download |

| many books |
| school uniforms |
| one's email |
| robots |
| yoga |
| us |
| music files |
| one's sister |

1 우리 선생님은 우리를 사랑하신다.

　—————————————————————————————

2 나는 그의 여동생을 안다.

　—————————————————————————————

3 Grace는 요가를 배운다.

　—————————————————————————————

4 Chris는 로봇들을 수집한다.

　—————————————————————————————

5 우리는 교복을 입는다.

　—————————————————————————————

6 Max와 Sue는 많은 책을 읽는다.

　—————————————————————————————

7 나는 매일 내 이메일을 확인한다.

　—————————————————————————————

8 우리는 음악 파일들을 다운로드 한다.

　—————————————————————————————

C 그림을 보고 보기에서 알맞은 단어를 찾아 좋아하는 것과 싫어하는 것에 대한 문장을 쓰시오.

| soccer　　meat　　vegetables　　baseball |

0 Minhee likes rabbits　　　　　　　　　　 .

　She hates hamsters.

1 1) Mike ————————————————————— .

　2) —————————————————————————————

2 1) Donna ———————————————————— .

　2) —————————————————————————————

WRAP UP

A 그림을 보고 보기에서 알맞은 표현을 찾아 가족을 소개하는 문장을 쓰시오.

a famous writer / slim	a basketball player / tall
a businessman / heavy	an elementary school student / short

0 I *am a middle school student* . *I am thin.*

1 My father _____ .

2 My mother _____ .

3 My brother _____ .

4 My sister _____ .

B 각 보기에서 알맞은 표현을 찾아 다음과 같이 문장을 쓰시오.

cook	teach	drive	play

soccer	English	a big bus	delicious food

0 Dana is a doctor. *She treats sick people.*

1 Jaeho is a good cook. _____

2 Ella is a driver. _____

3 Yunseok is a sportsman. _____

4 Kate is a teacher. _____

C 다음 우리말에 맞게 영어로 쓰시오.

1

Jessy는 여배우이다. (actress)

2

나는 새 휴대전화가 필요하다.

3

나는 한국어를 말한다.

4

나의 과학 수업은 재미있다. (science class)

5

Joey와 Sally는 무서운 영화를 좋아한다. (scary movies)

6

그녀의 이름은 Jane이다.

7

내 이웃들은 다정하다. (friendly)

8

나는 Andy의 이메일 주소를 안다. (email address)

D 다음 우리말에 맞게 영어로 쓰시오.

1

> Joan has two sisters. They are twins. 1) 그들은 비슷하다. 2) 그들은 같은 안경을 쓴다. They wear the same clothes, too.

1) _____ (similar)

2) _____ (glasses)

2

> I am from Gyeongju. 1) 경주는 작은 도시이다. But it is famous. It has many beautiful places. 2) 많은 사람들이 그 도시를 방문한다.

1) _____

2) _____

E 주어진 정보를 바탕으로 음식점 평가에 관한 글을 쓰시오.

0 **Arirang** ★★★★★ (*bulgogi* / delicious / fast)

Arirang has *bulgogi*.

Bulgogi is delicious.

The service is fast.

1 **Haru** ★★★★★ (sushi / fresh / kind)

1) _____

2) _____

3) _____

2 **Italiano** ★★★★★ (cheese pizza / bad / slow)

1) _____

2) _____

3) _____

F 다음과 같은 내용으로 펜팔 친구에게 자신을 소개하는 이메일을 쓰시오.

Name: Yuna   Age: 14   Likes: movies

Hi, John!
Nice to meet you.

1 _____

2 _____

3 _____

Yuna

LESSON 2

문장의 형식 II

neckache	skin	wizard	thirsty
secret	lie	regular	refrigerator
funny	angry	exercise	microwave
joke	novel	healthy	air cleaner
clock	genius	interesting	air conditioner
eraser	boring	excited	cousin
gift	convenient	tired	worry
bring	dishwasher	score	curtain
science	dish	glad	during
handsome	safe	blanket	bookworm

UNIT1 주어 + 동사 + 간접목적어 + 직접목적어

The small lamp gives me a neckache.

★ '~에게 …을 (-해)주다'를 표현하는 문장에서는 동사 뒤에 간접목적어 (~에게)와 직접목적어(…을)를 차례로 쓴다.

주어	+	동사	+	간접목적어	+	직접목적어

I give my cat food.
Hiroko teaches us Japanese.
Tom tells me his secrets.

> **Note**
> 수여동사는 '~에게(간접목적어)', '…을(직접목적어)'에 해당하는 두 개의 목적어를 취하는 동사이다.
> 예) give, buy, teach, send, show, lend, make, bring, ask, tell, write 등

A 괄호 안의 단어를 배열하여 올바른 문장으로 다시 쓰시오.

1 지희는 나에게 웃긴 농담을 말해준다. (tells, me, Jihee, funny jokes)

2 Lisa는 그녀의 아빠에게 케이크를 만들어 드린다. (a cake, makes, her dad, Lisa)

3 Ben은 그의 부모님께 질문을 한다. (questions, his parents, asks, Ben)

4 우리 엄마는 우리에게 피자를 사주신다. (buys, our mother, pizza, us)

5 시계는 우리에게 시간을 보여준다. (the time, a clock, us, shows)

6 나의 개는 나에게 뽀뽀를 해준다. (gives, a kiss, me, my dog)

7 민수는 나에게 그의 지우개를 빌려준다. (me, Minsu, lends, his eraser)

8 Cathy는 그녀의 할머니께 편지를 써드린다.
(Cathy, a letter, writes, her grandmother)

B 각 보기에서 알맞은 표현을 찾아 우리말에 맞게 영어로 쓰시오.

1 나의 조부모님은 나에게 선물들을 사주신다.

_____

2 Susan은 그녀의 친구들에게 생일카드들을 보내준다.

_____

3 나는 Rebecca에게 몇 가지 질문들을 한다.

_____

4 나의 여동생은 나에게 그녀의 옷을 빌려준다.

_____

5 웨이터들은 우리에게 음식을 가져다 준다.

_____

6 나의 할머니는 나에게 이야기를 말해주신다.

_____

7 나는 나의 남동생에게 저녁을 만들어 준다.

_____

lend
send
bring
ask
buy
make
tell

gifts
stories
some questions
one's clothes
food
birthday cards
dinner

C 그림을 보고 보기에서 알맞은 표현을 찾아 각 과목 선생님에 대한 문장을 쓰시오.

show   ask   some pictures of China   many questions

0

Ms. Kim teaches us math _____ .

She gives us a lot of homework.

1

1) Mr. Taylor _____ .

2) _____

2

1) Ms. Chung _____ .

2) _____

UNIT 2 주어 + 동사 + 목적어 + 목적보어

I am handsome.
*My blue skin **makes me** special.*

★ 목적어를 보충 설명하는 목적보어는 목적어 뒤에 쓴다.

주어	+	동사	+	목적어	+	목적보어

We **call** our cat Nero.
His lies **make** me angry.
Kate **keeps** her room warm.

A 괄호 안의 단어를 배열하여 올바른 문장으로 다시 쓰시오.

1 이 소설은 나를 슬프게 한다. (sad, makes, this novel, me)

2 우리는 그를 천재라고 부른다. (we, a genius, him, call)

3 사람들은 그 책이 지루하다는 것을 안다. (find, boring, the book, people)

4 컴퓨터는 생활을 편리하게 한다. (make, convenient, life, computers)

5 식기 세척기는 그릇을 깨끗하게 한다. (make, dishwashers, clean, dishes)

6 우리는 Harry Potter를 마법사라 부른다. (a wizard, call, we, Harry Potter)

7 그 알람은 당신의 집을 안전하게 지켜준다. (the alarm, safe, keeps, your house)

8 규칙적인 운동은 사람들을 건강하게 유지시킨다.
(regular exercise, healthy, keeps, people)

B 각 보기에서 알맞은 단어를 찾아 우리말에 맞게 영어로 쓰시오.

1 이 부츠는 내 발을 따뜻하게 유지해준다.

_____

2 이 사진은 나를 배고프게 한다.

_____

| call |
| make |
| keep |
| find |

3 사람들은 Daniel을 왕자라고 부른다.

_____

4 채소들은 우리를 건강하게 유지시킨다.

_____

5 사람들은 그 영화가 재미있다는 것을 안다.

_____

| a baby |
| clean |
| healthy |
| warm |
| hungry |
| interesting |
| a prince |

6 나의 부모님은 내 여동생을 아기라고 부르신다.

_____

7 우리는 우리 교실을 깨끗하게 유지한다.

_____

C 그림을 보고 괄호 안의 표현을 활용하여 기분을 좋게 하는 것과 나쁘게 하는 것에 대한 문장을 쓰시오.

0 (Saturdays, excited / Mondays, tired)

Saturdays make me excited.

Mondays make me tired.

1 (high test scores, happy / low test scores, sad)

1) _____

2) _____

2 (nice people, glad / bad people, angry)

1) _____

2) _____

WRAP UP

A 각 보기에서 알맞은 표현을 찾아 도움이 필요한 친구들에게 해줄 수 있는 일에 대해 쓰시오.

teach	give	lend	make

one's history textbook	a sandwich	water	English

0 Jane feels cold. *I bring her a blanket.*

1 Tim is thirsty. ....

2 Anne needs a history textbook. ....

3 Joe is hungry. ....

4 John's English score is bad. ....

B 그림을 보고 각 보기에서 알맞은 단어를 찾아 전자제품의 기능에 대한 문장을 쓰시오.

keep	make

clean	warm	cool	bright

0 A refrigerator *keeps food fresh* .

1 A microwave ....

2 An air cleaner ....

3 A lamp ....

4 An air conditioner ....

C 다음 우리말에 맞게 영어로 쓰시오.

1 _____

Jim은 그의 책상을 깨끗하게 유지한다.

2 _____

Mr. Jang은 우리에게 불어를 가르쳐 주신다. (French)

3 _____

그 드라마는 나를 슬프게 만든다. (drama)

4 _____

나는 나의 사촌들에게 크리스마스 카드들을 보낸다. (cousin)

5 _____

우리는 우리의 개를 Ron이라고 부른다.

6 _____

Lily는 그녀의 친구들에게 그녀의 고민들을 말한다. (worries)

7 _____

커튼은 방을 따뜻하게 유지시킨다. (curtains)

8 _____

June은 나에게 그녀의 책들을 빌려준다.

D 다음 우리말에 맞게 영어로 쓰시오.

1

Mr. Anderson is my teacher. 1) 그는 우리에게 역사를 가르쳐 주신다. 2) 그는 수업 중에 우리에게 재미있는 이야기들을 말해주신다. So, every student in my class likes him.

1) _____

2) _____ (during class)

2

Jack is my best friend. 1) 나는 그를 독서광이라고 부른다. He reads a lot of books. 2) 그는 나에게 많은 이야기를 말해준다. I like him.

1) _____ (bookworm)

2) _____

E　주어진 정보를 바탕으로 광고글을 쓰시오.

0　　　　　　　　**Golden Chocolate Shop**	
(a box of chocolate / boyfriend)	
Special Valentine's Day service!	
We make you a box of chocolate.	
We send your boyfriend this box of chocolate.	
1　　　　　　　　**Jenny's Cake Shop**	
(a cake / girlfriend)	
Special White Day service!	
1) _____	
2) _____	
2　　　　　　　　**May Flower Shop**	
(a flower basket / parents)	
Special Parents' Day service!	
1) _____	
2) _____	

F　보기에서 집에서 개를 기르는 것에 찬성하는 생각과 반대하는 생각에 해당하는 단어를 한 개씩 골라 그 찬성과 반대에 대한 문장을 쓰시오.

happy　　busy　　excited　　tired

agree

0　 I agree. A dog keeps our house safe.

1　 _____

disagree

0　 I disagree. A dog makes our house dirty.

2　 _____

LESSON 3

문장의 종류 Ⅰ

comfortable	beach	take a taxi	touch
shy	wash	stomachache	face
class	turn off	take medicine	dry
sleepy	order	score	expensive
difficult	eat out	online class	fight
save	police	healthy	waste
energy	noise	fast food	work
breakfast	correct	walk	carrot
cap	wrong	safe	onion
together	answer	mask	map

UNIT 1 부정문

I do not like this lamp.
It is not comfortable.

1 be동사의 부정: ⟨am[are, is] + not⟩
I **am not** shy.
Sue **is not** at home.

2 일반동사의 부정: ⟨do[does] not + 동사원형⟩
I **do not like** chocolate.
Jake **does not have** a class today.

A 문장을 다음과 같이 고쳐 쓰시오.

0 I am tired.
  I am not tired.

1 Jasmine is a cook.

2 I like rock music.

3 Aiden is from England.

4 Mike and James are basketball players.

5 They are my brothers.

6 Emma eats meat.

7 Paul and Judy have a lot of homework.

8 Lily watches movies.

26

B 각 보기에서 알맞은 표현을 찾아 우리말에 맞게 영어로 쓰시오.

		be
		like
		eat
		play
		save

1 나는 졸리지 않다.

_____

2 영어는 어렵지 않다.

_____

3 Harry는 에너지를 절약하지 않는다.

_____

4 나는 나의 짧은 머리를 좋아하지 않는다.

_____

5 Jim과 Henry는 내 반 친구가 아니다.

_____

6 나는 피아노를 치지 않는다.

_____

7 나의 아빠는 아침을 드시지 않는다.

_____

보기:
energy
breakfast
difficult
sleepy
one's classmates
one's short hair
the piano

C 괄호 안의 표현을 활용하여 전학 온 학생들을 묘사하는 문장을 쓰시오.

Kate   Nick   Hyori

0 Kate is not short . She does not wear glasses. (short / glasses)

1 Nick _____ . _____ (heavy / white pants)

2 Hyori _____ . _____ (thin / a cap)

UNIT 2 명령문

1 '~해라'라는 의미로 부탁이나 명령을 할 때 주어를 생략하고 동사원형을 쓴다.

Be quiet.　　　　　　　**Open** the door.

2 '~하지 마라'라는 의미의 명령문 부정은 명령문 앞에 Do not을 쓴다.

Do not be late.　　　　**Do not tell** a lie.

3 '~하자'라는 의미로 제안할 때 Let's 뒤에 동사원형을 쓴다.

Let's have lunch together.

4 '~하지 말자'라는 의미의 청유문 부정은 Let's 뒤에 not을 쓴다.

Let's not go to the beach.

A　괄호 안의 단어를 배열하여 올바른 문장으로 다시 쓰시오.

1 세수를 해라. (your face, wash)

2 네 친구에게 친절해라. (to your friends, kind, be)

3 내 방에 들어오지 마. (enter, do, my room, not)

4 콘서트에 가자. (go, let's, to the concert)

5 네 휴대전화를 꺼라. (your cell phone, turn off)

6 피자를 주문하자. (let's, a pizza, order)

7 오늘은 외식하지 말자. (not, eat out, let's, today)

8 수줍어하지 마라. (do, be, shy, not)

B 각 보기에서 알맞은 표현을 찾아 우리말에 맞게 영어로 쓰시오.

1 경찰을 불러라.
_____

2 소란스럽게 하지 마라.
_____

3 틀린 답들을 수정해라.
_____

4 영화를 보자.
_____

5 식당에서 뛰지 마라.
_____

6 한국 음식을 먹자.
_____

7 택시를 타지 말자.
_____

take
eat
make
correct
call
watch
run

the police
a taxi
noise
a movie
in the restaurant
the wrong answers
Korean food

C 그림을 보고 각 보기에서 알맞은 표현을 찾아 친구가 해야 할 것과 하지 말아야 할 것에 대해 쓰시오.

take   walk   play   eat
an online class   computer games   to school   fast food

0
You have a stomachache.

Do not eat ice cream.

Take some medicine.

1
Your test score is bad.

1) _____

2) _____

2
You are not healthy.

1) _____

2) _____

WRAP UP

A 그림을 보고 보기에서 알맞은 단어를 찾아 싫어하는 것과 그 이유에 대해 쓰시오.

math   medicine   delicious   easy

0

I do not like online shopping.

It is not safe.

1

1) _____

2) _____

2

1) _____

2) _____

B 그림을 보고 각 보기에서 알맞은 표현을 찾아 독감 예방법에 대해 쓰시오.

0   **1**   **2**   **3**

wash   drink   touch

a lot of water   one's hands   one's face

0   Wear a mask.

1   _____

2   _____

3   _____

C 다음 우리말에 맞게 영어로 쓰시오.

1

네 머리를 말려라. (dry)

2

그 스마트폰은 비싸지 않다.

3

싸우지 말자. (fight)

4

그들은 서울에 있지 않다. (in)

5

나는 그의 전화번호를 모른다.

6

너의 돈을 낭비하지 마라. (waste)

7

우리의 숙제를 시작하자.

8

이 컴퓨터는 작동하지 않는다. (work)

D 다음 우리말에 맞게 영어로 쓰시오.

1

My sister and I are very different. 1) 나는 당근을 먹지 않는다. I like onions.
2) 나의 여동생은 양파를 좋아하지 않는다. She likes carrots.

1) _____

2) _____

2

We need something for breakfast. 1) 슈퍼마켓에 가라. Buy some milk and bread.
We have a lot of juice. 2) 주스를 사지 마라.

1) _____

2) _____

E 주어진 정보를 바탕으로 환불 신청서를 쓰시오.

0

Item: a table
Reasons: design ☑   color ☐   size ☐

I do not like the design.
It is not pretty.

1

Item: a shirt
Reasons: design ☐   color ☑   size ☐

1) ....

2) ....

2

Item: a bag
Reasons: design ☐   color ☐   size ☑

1) ....

2) ....

F 함께 한라산을 등반할 친구에게 꼭 챙겨야 할 것에 대해 제안하려고 한다. 다음 제시된 그림을 보고,
주어진 어구를 활용하여 제안하는 메시지를 쓰시오.

0	1	2
- some water	- a map	- a camera

0 Let's take some water.

1 ....

2 ....

LESSON 4

문장의 종류 II

master	wish	hall	library
designer	birthday	station	grandparents
uncle	feel	dinner	scary
part-time job	come from	job	well
sitcom	subway	festival	close
exciting	hospital	club	vacation
too	favorite	playground	museum
busy	actor	title	holiday
address	restroom	singer	modern
climb	lunch	age	gallery

UNIT 1 의문사가 없는 의문문

Are you my master?

1 be동사의 의문문: 〈be동사 + 주어~?〉

Is Jihun handsome?

Are they your classmates?

2 일반동사의 의문문: 〈Do[Does] + 주어 + 동사원형~?〉

Do you have a girlfriend?

Does Andrew play computer games?

> **note**
>
> 의문사가 없는 의문문에 대한 대답은 Yes / No로 한다.
> Is Tom American?
> – **Yes**, he is. / **No**, he isn't.
> Do you know him?
> – **Yes**, I do. / **No**, I don't.

A 문장을 다음과 같이 고쳐 쓰시오.

0 You are a designer.

Are you a designer?

1 Your uncle lives in Busan.

2 Jonghee and Max are friends.

3 You have a part-time job.

4 The sitcom is exciting.

5 Jennifer goes to Seoul Middle School.

6 Eric is from Australia.

7 They go to school by bus.

8 This jacket is too big for Sam.

> *Tips for Writing*
>
> 의문문의 끝에는 항상 물음표(?)를 붙인다.

B 보기에서 알맞은 표현을 찾아 우리말에 맞게 영어로 쓰시오.

1 너는 지금 바쁘니?
   _____

2 Paul은 한국 음식을 좋아하니?
   _____

3 너는 아침을 먹니?
   _____

4 Mr. Anderson은 수학 선생님이시니?
   _____

5 Alex와 Jamie는 중국어를 공부하니?
   _____

6 이것이 너의 휴대전화니?
   _____

7 그가 나의 주소를 알고 있니?
   _____

breakfast
one's cell phone
Chinese
Korean food
a math teacher
busy
one's address

C 그림을 보고 주어진 대답에 알맞은 질문을 쓰시오.

0 *Is it big?*
   – Yes, it is big.
   Does it have legs?
   – No, it doesn't have legs.

1 1) _____
   – No, it is not white.
   2) _____
   – Yes, it climbs trees.

2 1) _____
   – Yes, it is small.
   2) _____
   – No, it doesn't have short ears.

UNIT 2 의문사가 있는 의문문

What is your wish?

1　be동사의 의문문: 〈의문사 + be동사 + 주어~?〉
Who are those boys?
When is Sue's birthday?

2　일반동사의 의문문: 〈의문사 + do[does] + 주어 + 동사원형~?〉
How do you feel now?
Where does John live?

note
....
의문사의 종류
who(누구), what(무엇),
when(언제), where(어디에),
why(왜), how(어떻게)

A　각 대답의 밑줄 친 부분을 묻는 질문을 쓰시오.

0　Where does Tim come from?

Tim comes from Hawaii.

1

I watch American dramas in the evening.

2

Valentine's Day is on February 14th.

3

Sam goes to school by subway.

4

Your cell phone is on the bed.

5

The hospital opens at 9:00 a.m.

6

My favorite actor is Andrew Garfield.

7

I want a hamburger for lunch.

8

The restroom is down the hall.

B 보기에서 알맞은 표현을 찾아 우리말에 맞게 영어로 쓰시오.

1 너의 음악 선생님은 누구시니?

   ....

2 너는 왜 여름을 좋아하니?

   ....

3 지하철역이 어디에 있습니까?

   ....

4 Sean은 언제 저녁을 먹니?

   ....

5 Emma의 직업은 무엇이니?

   ....

6 너는 어떻게 영어를 공부하니?

   ....

7 학교 축제는 언제니?

   ....

8 너는 왜 화났니?

   ....

English
summer
one's music teacher
angry
dinner
one's job
the school festival
the subway station

C 친구와 문자메시지를 주고 받고 있다. 대답에 알맞은 질문을 쓰시오.

0

Let's go to the tennis club after school.

Okay. *When does the club meet?*

The club meets at four o'clock.

Where do they play?

They play on the playground.

1

Let's watch a play tomorrow.

Cool. 1) ....

The title is *My Best Buddy*.

2) ....

It starts at 6:00 p.m.

2

Let's go to the concert this Saturday.

Good. 1) ....

The singer is IU.

2) ....

The concert hall is on Main Street.

WRAP UP

A   자기 소개를 보고 각 대답에 알맞은 질문을 쓰시오.

Name: Amy
Lives: New York
Age: 14
Family: 2 brothers
Likes: movies

Name: Andy
Lives: Chicago
Age: 13
Family: 1 sister
Likes: sports

0   Does Amy live in Chicago?

– No, she doesn't live in Chicago. She lives in New York.

1   _____

– Yes, he is thirteen years old.

2   _____

– No, she doesn't have a sister. She has two brothers.

3   _____

– Yes, he likes sports.

B   친구들이 주말에 주로 하는 일을 묻고 있다. 대답의 밑줄 친 부분을 묻는 질문을 쓰시오.

0   What does Anne clean on Saturdays?

– Anne cleans her room on Saturdays.

1   _____

– Tom goes to the library on Sundays.

2   _____

– Hyunwoo plays soccer on Saturdays.

3   _____

– Jenny goes to the cooking class on Sundays.

4   _____

– Suji meets her grandparents on Saturdays.

C 다음 우리말에 맞게 영어로 쓰시오.

1

그 영화는 무섭니? (scary)

2

Emily는 노래를 잘하니? (well)

3

너는 피자를 어떻게 만드니?

4

너의 친한 친구는 누구니? (close)

5

너는 왜 런던에 가니? (London)

6

너의 아버지는 어디에서 일하시니?

7

너는 방과 후에 무엇을 하니? (after school)

D 다음 우리말에 맞게 영어로 쓰시오.

1

> 1) 너 멕시코 음식을 좋아하니? I know a good Mexican restaurant. 2) 너는 Taco Hill을 아니? It is on Fifth Avenue. Let's eat there.

1) _____

2) _____

2

> Hi, Jinhee.
> 1) 너의 새 학교는 어때? I miss you. 2) 너의 방학은 언제 시작하니?
> Visit me on vacation.
> *Peter*

1) _____

2) _____

E 다음은 각 기관의 홈페이지에 자주 묻는 질문이다. 답변을 보고 알맞은 질문을 쓰시오.

0

● ● ●　　　　　　　　　**City Hall Library FAQs**

Q: When does the library open?

A: The library opens at 8:00 a.m.

Q: Is it open every day?

A: No, it is not open every day. It closes on Mondays.

1

● ● ●　　　　　　　　　**History Museum FAQs**

Q: 1) _____

A: The museum closes at 7:00 p.m.

Q: 2) _____

A: Yes, it is open on holidays.

2

● ● ●　　　　　　　　　**Modern Art Gallery FAQs**

Q: 1) _____

A: The gallery is on Park Street.

Q: 2) _____

A: No, it doesn't open at 8:30 a.m. It opens at 9:00 a.m.

F 친구의 생일 파티에 초대받아서 가려고 한다. 다음 제시된 그림을 보고 주어진 어구를 활용하여 생일 파티에 대해 묻는 문장을 쓰시오.

0

- start, the party

1

- be, the party

2

- want, for your birthday

0　When does the party start?

1　_____

2　_____

LESSON 5

문장의 확장

plate	slide	towel	put
bench	cave	basket	refrigerator
frog	bus stop	pancake	sky
sleep	wallet	pink	paper
end	zoo	comic book	young
parking lot	bottle	pet	wise
bank	rabbit	iguana	lake
weekend	leave	bat	active
seesaw	cushion	pencil case	on stage
swing	doll	bring	theater

UNIT 1 전치사구

I am in the lamp. I am here for 10,000 years.

★ 전치사는 명사 앞에 쓰이며 시간, 장소 등을 나타낸다.
The concert starts **at 6:30 p.m.**
Big Ben is **in London**.
The cookies are **on the plate**.

> **note**
> **1 시간을 나타내는 전치사**
> at(구체적인 시각), in(오전, 오후, 월, 계절, 연도), on(날짜, 요일, 특정한 날)
> **2 장소를 나타내는 전치사**
> in(~안에), at(~에), on(~위에), under(~아래에), by(~옆에), next to(~옆에)

A 괄호 안의 단어를 배열하여 올바른 문장으로 다시 쓰시오.

1 공이 벤치 아래에 있다. (under, a ball, the bench, is)

----

2 개구리들은 겨울에 잔다. (frogs, winter, sleep, in)

----

3 도서관에서 만나자. (the library, meet, let's, at)

----

4 내 수업은 4시 30분에 끝난다. (my class, 4:30, ends, at)

----

5 많은 차가 주차장에 있다. (are, many cars, the parking lot, in)

----

6 그 병원은 일요일에 문을 닫는다. (closes, on, the hospital, Sundays)

----

7 그 은행은 나의 집 옆에 있다. (my house, next to, is, the bank)

----

8 나의 아빠는 주말에 골프를 치신다. (on, plays, my father, weekends, golf)

----

9 내 가방은 책상 위에 있다. (is, the desk, on, my bag)

B   보기에서 알맞은 표현을 찾아 그림 속 인물들의 위치를 묘사한 문장을 쓰시오.

| the slide |
| the bench |
| the swing |

0   Subin is on the seesaw   .

1   Sam   .

2   Jason   .

3   Jungsu   .

UNIT 2 There is ~ / There are ~

There is a lamp in the cave.

★ '~가 있다'라는 의미를 나타낼 때 〈There is + 단수명사 / There are + 복수명사〉를 쓴다.

There is a cell phone on the sofa.
There is some water in the cup.
There are many people at the bus stop.

Note
셀 수 없는 명사는 단수 취급한다.
예) water, juice, milk 등

A   보기에서 알맞은 표현을 찾아 우리말에 맞게 영어로 쓰시오.

1   그 의자 위에 지갑이 있다.

_____

2   그 동물원에는 두 마리의 팬더가 있다.

_____

| two pandas |
| a bicycle |
| a wallet |

3   벤치 옆에 자전거가 있다.

_____

4   그 병 안에 주스가 조금 있다.

_____

5   우리 반에는 35명의 학생들이 있다.

_____

6   나무 아래에 토끼가 한 마리 있다.

_____

a rabbit
some juice
35 students

B   그림을 보고 주어진 표현을 활용하여 거실을 묘사하시오.

0   There are three cushions on the sofa.   (three cushions, the sofa)

1   _____   (two dolls, the TV)

2   _____   (some towels, the basket)

3   _____   (a dog, the chair)

UNIT 3 등위접속사

*I do magic for my master, **but** I don't do magic for myself.*

★ 등위접속사 and(첨가), but(대조), or(선택)는 단어와 단어, 구와 구, 절과 절을
연결할 때 쓴다.

Joan has pancakes **and** milk in the morning.

Insu likes Italian food, **but** he doesn't like Chinese food.

I want a white bag **or** a pink bag.

A 다음 두 문장을 and, but, or로 연결하여 한 문장으로 쓰시오.

1 My dog is cute. My dog is smart.

_____

2 Jamie leaves today. Jamie leaves tomorrow.

_____

3 I like basketball. I don't play it.

_____

4 His name is Ming. He is from China.

_____

5 Mark speaks Korean well. Dana speaks Korean well.

_____

6 Do you want hot chocolate? Do you want juice?

_____

7 I know his face. I don't know his name.

_____

8 Minji has two sisters. Minji has one brother.

_____

Tips for Writing

and나 but으로 절과 절을 연결할 때에 접속사 앞에 쉼표(,)를 사용하여 그 의미를 더욱 분명히 할 수 있다.

B 그림을 보고 괄호 안의 표현을 활용하여 두 사람의 공통점과 차이점에 대해 쓰시오.

0

Misun   Dan

(many books / comic books)

Misun and Dan read many books.

Misun reads comic books, but Dan doesn't read them.

1

Tom   Minju

(chocolate / chocolate cake)

1) _____

2) _____

2

Julie   Jiho

(pets / iguanas)

1) _____

2) _____

WRAP UP

A 그림을 보고 괄호 안의 단어를 활용하여 효정이의 방을 묘사한 문장을 쓰시오.

0 There is a cell phone on the desk.   (cell phone)

1 .... (cushion)

2 .... (bat)

3 .... (teddy bear)

B 그림을 보고 괄호 안의 표현을 활용하여 질문에 알맞은 대답을 쓰시오.

0

What do Soyoung and Alice eat for breakfast?
(bread, salad)

Soyoung eats bread and salad.

Alice eats bread, but she doesn't eat salad.

1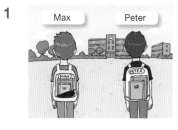

What do Max and Peter have in their bags?
(some books, a pencil case)

1) ....

2) ....

2

What do Olivia and Sumin bring to the party?
(pizza, Coke)

1) ....

2) ....

C 다음 우리말에 맞게 영어로 쓰시오.

1

내 생일은 5월이다.

2

James는 내 옆에 앉는다.

3

나는 그 테이블 위에 내 열쇠들을 둔다. (put)

4

냉장고 안에 우유가 있다. (refrigerator)

5

하늘에 많은 별이 있다. (in)

6

나는 지금 종이와 펜이 필요하다.

7

Mary는 어리지만, 그녀는 현명하다. (wise)

8

피자나 스파게티를 먹자. (spaghetti)

D 다음 우리말에 맞게 영어로 쓰시오.

1

> Many people visit this park in my town. It is beautiful. 1) 공원에는 큰 호수가 있다. There are also many trees and flowers. 2) 나무들에는 많은 새들이 있다.

1) _____ (lake)

2) _____ (in)

2

> 1) Jane과 Susan 친한 친구들이다. But they are very different. 2) Jane은 활발하지만, Susan은 조용하다. Jane likes sports, but Susan likes books.

1) _____ (close)

2) _____ (active)

E 주어진 정보를 바탕으로 연극 안내문을 쓰시오.

0

Play: *Code X*	*Code X* is on stage on June 23rd.
Date: June 23rd	
Time: 2:00 p.m.	It starts at 2:00 p.m.
Place: Main Theater	It is in the Main Theater.

1

Play: *Marine Boy*
Date: July 11th
Time: 3:00 p.m.
Place: AM Theater

1) _____

2) _____

3) _____

2

Play: *King Bear*
Date: May 24th
Time: 5:00 p.m.
Place: Seoul Art Center

1) _____

2) _____

3) _____

F 다음 그림을 보고 괄호 안의 단어를 활용하여 진수의 책상을 묘사한 문장을 쓰시오.

This is Jinsu's desk.

1 _____ (box)

2 _____ (soccer ball)

3 _____ (book)

SECTION 2
GRAMMAR FOR WRITING

LESSON 6

시제 I

---

rub	laugh	wear	ago
last	romantic	sweater	fix
surf	fantastic	headache	trip
round	sunny	order	seafood
take a test	exercise	present	there
model plane	bakery	learn	activity
a lot	move	late for	farm
horror	finish	break	ride
scream	pass	travel	sunset
comedy	join	build	fast

UNIT 1 과거시제

Hooray! Somebody **rubbed** the lamp.

★ '~했다, ~이었다'라는 의미로 과거의 상태나 한 일을 나타낼 때 동사의
과거형을 쓴다.
I **was** busy yesterday.
They **were** in Busan last week.
Harry **called** me last night.

note

현재의 사실 · 상태, 일상적인
습관 · 동작, 불변의 사실을 나타낼 때
현재시제를 쓴다.
I **live** in Korea.
He **surfs** the Internet every day.
The Earth **is** round.

A 문장을 다음과 같이 고쳐 쓰시오.

0 Tom lives in New York.

Tom lived in New York.

1 I make a sandwich for my parents.

2 His birthday is on Saturday.

3 They go to the mall after school.

4 Mr. Smith is my homeroom teacher.

5 Lisa and I are in the theater.

6 The concert starts at 7:00 p.m.

7 There are many people at the station.

8 I take a science test this afternoon.

B 그림을 보고 각 보기에서 알맞은 단어를 찾아 과거에 한 일에 대한 문장을 쓰시오.

0	1	2	3
yesterday	last weekend	last Tuesday	yesterday

make   visit   buy

one's grandparents   a model plane   a smartphone

0 Sean *cooked spaghetti yesterday* .

1 Jonghee _____ .

2 Amy _____ .

3 Matt _____ .

C 주어진 표현을 활용하여 영화 감상에 대한 문장을 쓰시오.

0
- horror movie
  - scary
  - scream

I watched a horror movie.

It was scary.

I screamed a lot.

1
- comedy
  - funny
  - laugh

1) _____

2) _____

3) _____

2
- romantic movie
  - sad
  - cry

1) _____

2) _____

3) _____

UNIT 2 미래시제

I will show you my fantastic magic.

★ '~할 것이다'라는 의미로 미래의 일을 예측하거나, 앞으로의 계획 또는 의지를
  나타낼 때 ⟨will + 동사원형⟩을 쓴다.
  It **will be** sunny tomorrow.
  Junhee **will go** to Rome next month.
  I **will exercise** every morning.

A 괄호 안의 표현을 활용하여 문장을 다음과 같이 고쳐 쓰시오.

0 I get up early in the morning.

I will get up early in the morning.

Tips for Writing

3인칭 단수를 주어로 하는 현재시제 문장을 미래시제로 바꿀 경우, 동사에서 –(e)s를 떼는 것에 유의해야 한다.

1 A new bakery opens this month.

_____

2 We watch movies on Saturday.

_____

3 My family moves to Daejeon. (next year)

_____

4 I help you with your homework. (tomorrow)

_____

5 Jaemin comes to my birthday party. (next week)

_____

6 This concert ends at ten o'clock.

_____

7 Sujin takes yoga classes. (next month)

_____

8 We are high school students. (next year)

_____

B 각 보기에서 알맞은 표현을 찾아 우리말에 맞게 영어로 쓰시오.

1 나는 내일 그 일을 끝낼 것이다.

_____

2 나는 이번 주말에 이 책들을 읽을 것이다.

_____

3 Monica는 다음 달에 빨간 차를 살 것이다.

_____

4 Brian은 화요일에 그의 친구들을 만날 것이다.

_____

5 Michael은 수학 시험을 통과할 것이다.

_____

6 나는 테니스 동아리에 가입할 것이다.

_____

7 우리는 오후 1시에 중국 음식을 먹을 것이다.

_____

meet
pass
read
buy
join
eat
finish

one's friends
the work
Chinese food
these books
the tennis club
a red car
the math test

C 그림을 보고 주어진 단어를 활용하여 그림 속 인물들이 앞으로 할 일에 대한 문장을 쓰시오.

0

- close   - wear

Minji is cold.

She will close the window.

She will wear a sweater.

1

- see   - go

Junhyun has a headache.

1) _____

2) _____

2

- make   - order

Ron is hungry.

1) _____

2) _____

WRAP UP

A   다음은 혜진이의 생일 파티의 모습이다. 그림과 블로그를 보고 질문에 알맞은 대답을 쓰시오.

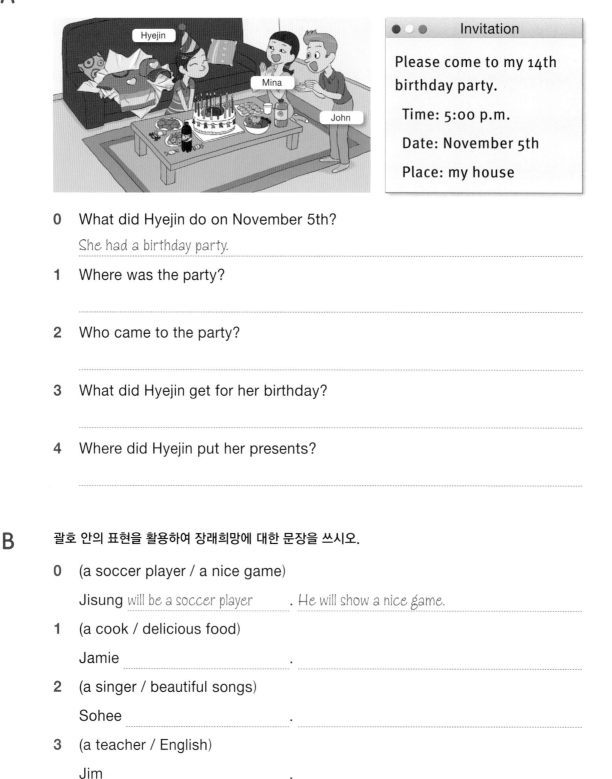

0   What did Hyejin do on November 5th?

She had a birthday party.

1   Where was the party?

2   Who came to the party?

3   What did Hyejin get for her birthday?

4   Where did Hyejin put her presents?

B   괄호 안의 표현을 활용하여 장래희망에 대한 문장을 쓰시오.

0   (a soccer player / a nice game)

Jisung will be a soccer player . He will show a nice game.

1   (a cook / delicious food)

Jamie

2   (a singer / beautiful songs)

Sohee

3   (a teacher / English)

Jim

C 다음 우리말에 맞게 영어로 쓰시오.

1

Tony와 나는 친한 친구들이었다. (close)

2

나는 다음 달에 태권도를 배울 것이다. (taekwondo)

3

Ted는 그의 엄마에게 꽃을 좀 사드렸다. (some)

4

Anne은 학교에 늦을 것이다. (late for)

5

내 여동생이 어제 내 휴대전화를 고장 냈다. (break)

6

나의 가족은 이번 주말에 부산으로 여행을 갈 것이다. (travel)

7

나의 할아버지는 50년 전에 우리 집을 지으셨다. (ago)

8

Mike가 내일 내 컴퓨터를 고쳐 줄 것이다. (fix)

D 다음 우리말에 맞게 영어로 쓰시오.

1

> Lucy visited Sokcho with her family. 1) 그녀는 아름다운 해변에 갔다. 2) 그녀는 그 곳에서 많은 해산물을 먹었다. It was a nice trip.

1) _____

2) _____ (seafood, there)

2

> 1) 나는 이번 토요일에 바쁠 것이다. In the morning, I will finish my English homework. After that, I will meet my friends. 2) 우리는 공원에서 농구를 할 것이다.

1) _____

2) _____

E 다음은 제주도 여행 일정표이다. 일정표를 보고 여행 일정 안내문을 쓰시오.

Time	Place	Activity
9:00 a.m. ~12:00 p.m.	the Teddy Bear Museum	see cute teddy bears
2:00 p.m. ~ 5:00 p.m.	the horse farm	ride a horse
5:00 p.m. ~ 6:30 p.m.	Suwolbong Peak	watch the sunset

JEJU TOUR PACKAGE

9:00 a.m. ~ 12:00 p.m.

You will go to the Teddy Bear Museum.

You will see cute teddy bears there.

2:00 p.m. ~ 5:00 p.m.

1 _____

2 _____

5:00 p.m. ~ 6:30 p.m.

3 _____

4 _____

F 주어진 표현을 활용하여 그림 1, 2, 3이 나타내는 상황을 각각 묘사하는 문장을 쓰시오.

1
- wake up
- this morning

2
- run
- fast

3
- miss
- the school bus

1 Gwangsu _____ .

2 _____

3 But _____ .

LESSON 7

시제 II

wait for	gym	wash dishes	move
diary	essay	take a walk	blow up
stay	take a shower	sunglasses	balloon
in line	brush	kick	French
chat	tooth	newspaper	smile
pool	raincoat	classroom	paint
update	kid	slow down	wall
sand castle	stage	turn off	living room
lie	climb	sweep	leaf
volleyball	mountain	floor	little

UNIT 1 현재진행형

I am waiting for a wish.

★ '~하고 있다'라는 의미로 현재에 진행 중인 일을 표현할 때 〈am[are, is] + v-ing〉를 쓴다.

I **am reading** an email.
He **is talking** on the phone.
They **are playing** soccer on the playground.

A 문장을 다음과 같이 고쳐 쓰시오.

0 I write in my diary.

    I am writing in my diary.

1 We stay in London.

2 Minhye stands in line.

3 I chat online with my friend.

4 The boys play baseball.

5 My brother uses my smartphone.

6 They swim in the pool.

7 Joe and Karen eat sandwiches in the kitchen.

8 Jenny updates her blog.

B 각 보기에서 알맞은 표현을 찾아 그림 속 인물들의 행동을 묘사한 문장을 쓰시오.

play	lie	eat	build

ice cream	a sand castle	volleyball	on the towel

0 Daniel is swimming in the sea   .

1 Eunji   .

2 Sarah   .

3 Mike   .

4 Steve and Jimin   .

C 친구와 문자메시지를 주고 받고 있다. 주어진 표현을 활용하여 알맞은 문장을 쓰시오.

0

- watch a sitcom
- eat lunch with Sam

I am watching a sitcom.

What are you doing?

I am eating lunch with Sam.

1

- study for a math test
- exercise at the gym

1) _____

What are you doing?

2) _____

2

- bake a birthday cake
- write an essay

1) _____

2) _____

3) _____

UNIT 2 과거진행형

I am sorry. I am late. I **was taking** a shower.

★ '~하고 있었다'라는 의미로 과거에 진행 중인 일을 표현할 때 〈was[were] + v-ing〉를 쓴다.

I **was brushing** my teeth.
Sumin **was wearing** a raincoat.
The kids **were playing** with a ball.

A 문장을 다음과 같이 고쳐 쓰시오.

0 I had dinner with my family.

I was having dinner with my family.

1 Amy listened to music in her room.

_____

2 Minsik and I danced on the stage.

_____

3 I waited for Seungho.

_____

4 They had a birthday party.

_____

5 My parents climbed a mountain.

_____

6 I fixed my computer.

_____

7 Jina washed dishes in the kitchen.

_____

8 David and Sue took a walk.

_____

B 각 보기에서 알맞은 표현을 찾아 우리말에 맞게 영어로 쓰시오.

1 Luke는 이메일을 쓰고 있었다.

_____

2 나는 나의 영어책을 찾고 있었다.

_____

3 그녀는 선글라스를 쓰고 있었다.

_____

4 Joe와 나는 공을 차고 있었다.

_____

5 나의 아빠는 신문을 읽고 계셨다.

_____

6 우리는 교실을 청소하고 있었다.

_____

7 나의 엄마는 쿠키를 굽고 계셨다.

_____

| clean |
| write |
| bake |
| kick |
| look for |
| wear |
| read |

| the classroom |
| sunglasses |
| a newspaper |
| cookies |
| one's English book |
| an email |
| a ball |

C 표를 보고 친구들이 일요일 오전 10시와 오후 3시에 하고 있었던 일에 대한 문장을 쓰시오.

	Mina	Sean	Jane
10:00 a.m.	take an online class	play the violin	play with her cat
3:00 p.m.	watch a movie	clean his room	watch a baseball game

0 Mina was taking an online class at 10:00 a.m.

She was watching a movie at 3:00 p.m.

1 1) Sean _____ .

2) _____

2 1) Jane _____ .

2) _____

WRAP UP

A 상황에 맞게 각 보기에서 알맞은 표현을 찾아 문장을 완성하시오.

wait for   drive   use

too fast   you   the computer

0 Be quiet. The baby *is sleeping*   .

1 I _____ . Don't turn it off.

2 Slow down. You _____ .

3 Hurry up! Your friends _____ .

B 다음은 교실에서 파티를 준비하는 모습이다. 보기에서 알맞은 단어를 찾아 질문에 알맞은 대답을 쓰시오.

blow up   write   move

0 Who was sweeping the floor?

Katie was sweeping the floor.

_____

1 What were Kara and Jay doing?

_____

_____

2 Who was blowing up a balloon?

_____

_____

3 What was Tiffany doing?

_____

_____

64

C 다음 우리말에 맞게 영어로 쓰시오.

1

나는 지금 불어를 공부하고 있다. (French)

2

그 아기는 미소 짓고 있었다.

3

Ann은 그녀의 엄마와 이야기하고 있다.

4

Carter와 Jason은 배드민턴을 치고 있었다. (badminton)

5

Terry는 그의 방에서 노래를 부르고 있다.

6

Sophie는 모자를 쓰고 있었다. (cap)

7

나의 형은 벽을 페인트칠하고 있다. (wall)

8

그는 카페테리아에서 점심을 먹고 있었다. (cafeteria)

D 다음 우리말에 맞게 영어로 쓰시오.

1

All my family is at home now. I am studying math. 1) 나의 아빠는 거실을 청소하고 계신다. My mother is cooking in the kitchen. 2) 나의 남동생은 그의 방에서 컴퓨터 게임을 하고 있다.

1)

2)

2

I called Jill and Amy this afternoon, but they didn't answer. 1) Jill은 집에서 자고 있었다. 2) Amy는 도서관에서 공부를 하고 있었다.

1)

2)

E 그림을 보고 동물원에서 본 동물들에 관한 일기를 쓰시오.

1

May 5th, Saturday ☀

Today I saw lots of animals at the zoo.
A panda was sleeping in a tree.

1) _____

It was very fun.

2

July 22nd, Saturday ☀

Today I saw lots of animals at the zoo.

1) _____

2) _____

It was very fun.

F 다음 그림을 보고 보기에서 알맞은 단어를 찾아 공원에 있는 등장인물들의 행동을 묘사한 문장을 쓰시오.

sandwiches a book a bike

There are some people at the park.

Two girls **1** _____ .

A little boy **2** _____ .

A tall woman **3** _____ .

LESSON 8

조동사

kill	borrow	save	turn on
skate	textbook	truth	solve
backpack	bring	fasten	dictionary
attend	cross	seat belt	gallery
meeting	street	trip	rule
carry	ride	map	area
alone	apologize	helmet	tube
keep	spend	hiking boots	palace
try on	wisely	on time	view
discount	promise	during	cheap

UNIT 1 능력을 나타내는 can, be able to

*I **can do** many things for my master, but I **cannot kill** people.*

★ '~할 수 있다'라는 의미의 능력을 나타낼 때 〈can + 동사원형〉 또는
〈be able to + 동사원형〉을 쓴다.

I **can bake** an apple pie.   Sue **can drive** a car.
Maria **is able to ride** a skateboard.   Jay **is able to skate** well.

A   문장을 다음과 같이 고쳐 쓰시오.

0   My little sister walks.

My little sister can walk.

1   I buy the backpack.

_____

2   My uncle fixes the computer.

_____

3   James and Suman ride horses.

_____

4   Hyunji cooks Italian food.

_____

5   They attend the meeting.

_____

6   I carry this heavy box alone.

_____

7   We read a book in English.

_____

8   Sally and Jack write in Chinese.

_____

9   Jinsu sings pop songs.

_____

B 보기에서 알맞은 단어를 찾아 그림 속 인물들의 능력에 대한 문장을 쓰시오.

0	1	2	3
- Eugene	- Sarah	- Jongmin	- Amy and Insu

tennis   a bike   the violin

0 Eugene is able to swim in the sea.

1 ....

2 ....

3 ....

UNIT 2 허가를 나타내는 can, may

Master, you may make three wishes.

★ '~해도 된다'라는 의미의 허가를 나타낼 때 〈can[may] + 동사원형〉을 쓴다.
You **can use** my cell phone.   You **can have** my pen.
You **may keep** this book for two weeks.   You **may sit** here.

A 문장을 다음과 같이 고쳐 쓰시오.

0 You try on this hat.
     You may try on this hat.

1 You use student discounts.

....

2 You call me Joe.

....

3 Kate borrows my textbook.

....

4 You sit next to me.

_____

5 You play computer games for thirty minutes.

_____

6 You play the piano in the room.

_____

B 그림을 보고 각 보기에서 알맞은 단어를 찾아 허가하는 내용의 문장을 쓰시오.

cross	ride	bring

the rides	one's pet	the street

0 You may come in.

1 _____

2 _____

3 _____

UNIT 3 의무 · 충고를 나타내는 should

You **should choose** your wishes carefully.

★ '~해야 한다'라는 의미의 의무 · 충고를 나타낼 때 〈should + 동사원형〉을 쓴다.
You **should apologize** to him.
We **should spend** our money wisely.
You **should keep** your promise.

A 각 보기에서 알맞은 표현을 찾아 우리말에 맞게 영어로 쓰시오.

drink
finish
fasten
tell
save

the work
one's seat belt
a lot of water
energy
the truth

0 너는 빨간 불에서 멈춰야 한다.

You should stop at red lights.

1 우리는 에너지를 절약해야 한다.

_____

2 나는 오늘 그 일을 끝내야 한다.

_____

3 너는 많은 물을 마셔야 한다.

_____

4 우리는 진실을 말해야 한다.

_____

5 너는 네 안전벨트를 착용해야 한다.

_____

B 그림을 보고 주어진 표현을 활용하여 충고하는 내용의 문장을 쓰시오.

0

- a taxi / the people

Jackson will be late for the meeting.

He should take a taxi.

He should call the people.

1

- a map / a helmet

Mia will go on a bicycle trip.

1) _____

2) _____

2

- one's hiking boots / some water

Ron will climb a mountain.

1) _____

2) _____

WRAP UP

A 각 보기에서 알맞은 표현을 찾아 각 캐릭터의 능력을 나타내는 문장을 쓰시오.

0	1	2	3
- Peter Pan	- Tarzan	- Po	- Spiderman

talk with	climb	do

walls	animals	kung fu

0 Peter Pan can fly in the sky.

1 _____

2 _____

3 _____

B 괄호 안의 표현을 활용하여 학생들이 수업시간에 지켜야 하는 규칙에 대한 문장을 쓰시오.

0 (be, on time)

You should be on time for classes.

1 (turn off, one's cell phone)

_____ during classes.

2 (not, eat, any food)

_____

3 (bring, one's textbook)

_____

4 (not, chat, with one's classmates)

_____

C 다음 우리말에 맞게 영어로 쓰시오.

1

그들은 빠르게 달릴 수 있다.

2

너는 오늘 밤 Sam의 생일 파티에 가도 된다.

3

너는 천천히 운전해야 한다. (slowly)

4

나는 플루트를 연주할 수 있다. (flute)

5

네가 히터를 켜도 된다. (turn on, heater)

6

너는 매일 운동해야 한다.

7

그녀는 그 수학 문제를 풀 수 있다. (solve, math problem)

8

네가 내 게임 CD를 빌려가도 된다.

D 다음 우리말에 맞게 영어로 쓰시오.

1

Let's start the writing test. 1) 여러분은 여러분의 사전을 사용해도 됩니다. After the test, 2) 여러분은 집에 가셔도 됩니다. Do your best.

1) _____ (dictionary)

2) _____

2

It will rain this afternoon. 1) 너는 우산을 가지고 가야 한다. The traffic will be heavy. 2) 너는 지하철을 타야 한다.

1) _____ (bring)

2) _____ (take)

E 다음은 공공 장소의 규칙들이다. 그림을 보고 주어진 표현을 활용하여 규칙을 쓰시오.

1

Gallery Rule

You should stand behind the line. (stand)

1) _____ (pictures)

2) You may _____ . (photos)

2

Swimming Pool Rule

1) _____ (a swimming cap)

2) _____ (in the pool area)

3) _____ (a tube)

F 한국을 방문하는 외국인 친구에게 꼭 가봐야 할 곳을 추천하려고 한다. 그림을 보고 주어진 어구를 활용하여 추천하는 메시지를 쓰시오.

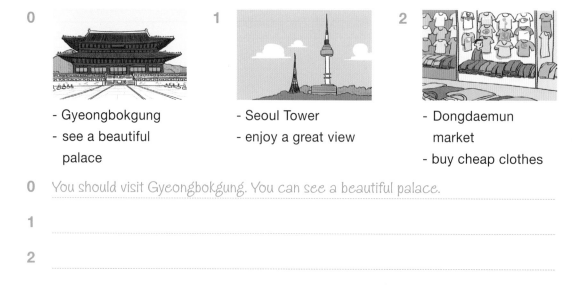

0
- Gyeongbokgung
- see a beautiful palace

1
- Seoul Tower
- enjoy a great view

2
- Dongdaemun market
- buy cheap clothes

0 You should visit Gyeongbokgung. You can see a beautiful palace.

1 _____

2 _____

LESSON 9
to부정사와 동명사

get out of	goal	mind	abroad
cave	golfer	expect	poor
plan	hobby	promise	cousin
carpet	win	practice	book report
abroad	surf	avoid	contest
dream	take a picture	give up	support
bakery	keep	throw	prize
decide	enjoy	director	go on a diet
fashion	astronaut	design	lose
join	dangerous	plane	electric

UNIT1 명사적 용법의 to부정사

*My master wants **to get** out of this cave.*
*My plan is **to make** him a flying carpet.*

★ 〈to + 동사원형〉 형태인 to부정사는 명사처럼 문장 내에서 주어, 보어,
목적어로 쓰일 수 있다.

To travel abroad is exciting. (주어)
My dream is **to open** a bakery. (보어)
I want **to be** a famous actor. (목적어)

> **Note**
> to부정사가 주어로 쓰일 때 3인칭
> 단수로 취급한다.

A 괄호 안의 단어를 배열하여 올바른 문장으로 다시 쓰시오.

1 Sam은 태권도를 배우기로 결심했다. (learn, Sam, to, decided, taekwondo)

----

2 내 직업은 컴퓨터를 수리하는 것이다. (to, a computer, my job, fix, is)

----

3 친구들과 이야기하는 것은 재미있다. (talk, to, fun, with friends, is)

----

4 내 계획은 오늘 그 일을 끝내는 것이다. (to, the work, today, finish, is, my plan)

----

5 일찍 일어나는 것은 쉽지 않다. (to, not, early, is, wake up, easy)

----

6 태민이는 록음악 듣는 것을 좋아한다.
(listen to, Taemin, to, likes, rock music)

----

7 그녀의 소원은 아름다운 집을 사는 것이다.
(is, a beautiful house, her wish, buy, to)

----

8 나는 내가 가장 좋아하는 가수를 만나기를 희망한다.
(I, meet, hope, my favorite singer, to)

B 보기에서 알맞은 표현을 찾아 우리말에 맞게 영어로 쓰시오.

1 내 꿈은 파리에서 패션을 공부하는 것이다.

_____

2 나는 새 자전거를 사기를 원한다.

_____

3 새로운 사람들을 만나는 것은 즐겁다.

_____

4 Katie는 영화 동호회에 가입하길 희망한다.

_____

5 Jay의 목표는 훌륭한 골프 선수가 되는 것이다.

_____

> join the movie club
> meet new people
> study fashion
> buy a new bike
> be a good golfer

UNIT 2 동명사

Flying on the carpet is exciting.

★ 〈동사원형 + ing〉 형태인 동명사는 명사처럼 문장 내에서 주어, 보어, 목적어로
쓰일 수 있다.
Telling a lie is wrong. (주어)
My hobby is **baking** cookies. (보어)
I enjoy **meeting** friends. (목적어)

> **note**
> 동명사가 주어로 쓰일 때 3인칭
> 단수로 취급한다.

A 괄호 안의 단어를 배열하여 올바른 문장으로 다시 쓰시오.

1 축구를 하는 것은 재미있다. (fun, playing, is, soccer)

_____

2 Dan의 목표는 금메달을 따는 것이다. (is, Dan's goal, the gold medal, winning)

_____

3 나는 인터넷 검색하는 것을 좋아한다. (like, I, the Internet, surfing)

_____

4 내 취미는 사진 찍는 것이다. (is, pictures, my hobby, taking)

_____

5 애완동물을 기르는 것은 쉽지 않다. (is, keeping, not, easy, a pet)

_____

6 Anne은 어제 쇼핑을 가지 않았다. (go, Anne, shopping, yesterday, didn't)

_____

B 보기에서 알맞은 표현을 찾아 우리말에 맞게 영어로 쓰시오.

1 Jerry는 시트콤 보는 것을 즐겼다.

_____

2 그의 꿈은 우주 비행사가 되는 것이다.

_____

| drink coffee |
| be an astronaut |
| watch sitcoms |
| drive fast |

3 빨리 운전하는 것은 위험하다.

_____

4 나의 엄마는 커피 마시는 것을 좋아하신다.

_____

UNIT 3 to부정사 vs. 동명사

My master **wishes to be** a prince.
I don't **mind doing** magic for him.

1 to부정사만을 목적어로 취하는 동사: want, hope, expect, wish, decide, plan, promise, need 등
I **hope to have** a cute dog.
We **expected to win** the baseball game.

2 동명사만을 목적어로 취하는 동사: enjoy, mind, finish, keep, practice, avoid, stop, give up 등
I **finished doing** my homework.
The baby **kept crying**.

> **Note**
> to부정사와 동명사를 둘 다 목적어로 취하는 동사(의미상 차이 없음): begin, start, like, love, hate 등
> I **like to draw** pictures.
> I **like drawing** pictures.

A 보기에서 알맞은 표현을 찾아 우리말에 맞게 영어로 쓰시오.

bring one's camera
learn Chinese
throw the ball
go to Spain
fix one's phone
buy a new wallet
drink Coke

1 나는 이번 겨울에 스페인에 갈 계획이다.

_____

2 너는 새 지갑을 살 필요가 있다.

_____

3 Tom은 그의 전화기를 고치는 것을 끝마쳤다.

_____

4 Eva는 내일 그녀의 카메라를 가지고 오기로 약속했다.

_____

5 그녀는 콜라를 마시는 것을 피했다.

_____

6 나는 중국어를 배우기로 결심했다.

_____

7 David는 공을 던지는 것을 연습했다.

_____

B 주어진 표현을 활용하여 좋아하는 것과 장래희망에 대해 쓰시오.

0
- watch movies
- a movie director

Peter *enjoys watching movies*   .

He wants to be a movie director.

1
- bake bread and
  cookies
- a baker

1) Marie _____ .

2) _____

2
- design clothes
- a fashion designer

1) Andre _____ .

2) _____

WRAP UP

A 그림을 보고 보기에서 알맞은 단어를 찾아 질문에 알맞은 대답을 쓰시오.

0	1	2	3

a plane ticket	mountains	New Zealand

0 What is your plan this summer?

My plan is to go abroad.

1 Where did you decide to go?

2 What do you need to do?

3 What do you want to do there?

B 보기에서 알맞은 단어를 찾아 두 문장의 의미가 비슷하도록 문장을 다시 쓰시오.

plan	enjoy	hope

0 Katie did all her homework.

Katie finished doing her homework.

1 Jongsu loves to make model planes.

2 Jay will stay in Rome for a day.

3 Yongmin's dream is to play soccer in the Premier League.

C 다음 우리말에 맞게 영어로 쓰시오.

1

작가가 되는 것이 나의 꿈이다.

2

Brian은 액션 영화 보는 것을 즐긴다. (action movies)

3

그녀의 직업은 일본어를 가르치는 것이다. (Japanese)

4

John은 가난한 사람들을 돕기를 원한다. (poor)

5

나는 이번 주말에 나의 사촌을 방문할 계획이다.

6

Patrick은 그 퍼즐을 푸는 것을 끝냈다. (solve, puzzle)

7

내 숙제는 독후감을 쓰는 것이다. (book report)

D 다음 우리말에 맞게 영어로 쓰시오.

1

Andy has a piano contest next Friday. 1) 그의 목표는 1등상을 타는 것이다.
2) 그는 매일 피아노 연주하기를 연습한다. His family is also supporting his goal.

1) _____ (win, first prize)

2) _____

2

Jungmi decided to go on a diet. 1) 그녀는 패스트푸드를 먹는 것을 멈췄다. 2) 그녀는
운동하기를 시작했다. Then, she was able to lose 2 kg in two weeks.

1) _____

2) _____

E 주어진 정보를 바탕으로 동아리 신청서를 쓰시오.

0

- **club:** movie club
- **likes:** watch movies
- **wishes:** see many movies

Name: Kim Sungho

I want to join the movie club.

I enjoy watching movies.

I wish to see many movies.

1

- **club:** hip hop dance club
- **likes:** dance
- **wishes:** learn hip hop dance

Name: Lee Minji

1) _____

2) _____

3) _____

2

- **club:** rock band
- **likes:** play the guitar
- **wishes:** play the electric guitar well

Name: Park Sejin

1) _____

2) _____

3) _____

F 이번 여름 방학에 여행을 가려고 한다. 주어진 단어나 어구를 활용하여 가려고 하는 나라와 그곳에서 하고 싶은 일을 쓰시오.

0

- China
- climb the Great Wall of China

1

- Australia
- see kangaroos

2

- Switzerland
- eat fondue

0 My plan is to visit China this summer. I want to climb the Great Wall of China.

1 _____

2 _____

LESSON 10

대명사 it

sunny	honest	unhealthy	change
outside	important	vegetable	habit
cloudy	solve	fruit	scary
dark	impossible	convenient	amusement park
bright	hard	toothpaste	ride
humid	machine	possible	begin
windy	lucky	protect	snowball fight
escape	helmet	finger	boring
danger	present	alone	thick
necessary	jog	promise	carry

UNIT1 비인칭 주어 it

It is summer now.
It is hot in the lamp.

★ 날씨, 시간, 요일, 날짜, 계절, 밝고 어두움, 거리 등을 표현할 때 비인칭 주어 it을 쓴다.

It is sunny outside.   **It** is ten o'clock now.
It is Friday.   **It** is June 18th.
It is spring.   **It** is dark in the room.
It is seven kilometers.

A   괄호 안의 내용이 답이 되도록 문장을 쓰시오.

1   What time is it now?

_____ (four twenty)

2   What day is it today?

_____ (Wednesday)

3   When is your birthday?

_____ (August 14th)

4   How is the weather today?

_____ (cloudy)

5   How far is it from your house to school?

_____ (500 meters)

6   What season is it?

_____ (summer)

7   How is it outside now?

_____ (dark)

8   How was the weather last summer?

_____ (rain a lot)

9   What is today's date?

_____ (September 1st)

B 보기에서 알맞은 표현을 찾아 우리말에 맞게 영어로 쓰시오.

1 오전 9시 30분이다.
_____

2 한국은 가을이다.
_____

3 오늘은 10월 15일이다.
_____

4 어제는 일요일이었다.
_____

5 이번 주말에 눈이 올 것이다.
_____

6 여기는 밝다.
_____

7 새해 첫날이다.
_____

Sunday
New Year's Day
snow
bright
October 15th
nine thirty
fall

C 주어진 정보를 활용하여 같은 시간대의 세계 각 도시의 날짜, 시각, 날씨에 대해 쓰시오.

0　　**Seoul**

July 25th
6:00 a.m.
hot and humid

It is July 25th.

It is six o'clock in the morning.

It is hot and humid.

1　　**New York**

July 24th
5:00 p.m.
hot and sunny

1) _____

2) _____

3) _____

2　　**Sydney**

July 25th
7:00 a.m.
cold and windy

1) _____

2) _____

3) _____

UNIT 2 가주어 it

It is his second wish to escape from danger.

★ to부정사구가 주어일 때 보통 주어 자리에 가주어 it을 쓰고, to부정사구는 문장 끝으로 보낸다.

It is great *to have a good friend*.
It is interesting *to learn new things*.
It is dangerous *to swim in the sea*.

A 문장을 다음과 같이 고쳐 쓰시오.

0 To play soccer is exciting.

　　It is exciting to play soccer.

1 To tell lies is bad.

_____

2 To talk with friends is fun.

_____

3 To read comic books is interesting.

_____

4 To keep your room clean is necessary.

_____

5 To be honest is important.

_____

6 To solve this problem was impossible.

_____

7 To find your house was hard.

_____

8 To use this machine is great.

_____

B 각 보기에서 알맞은 표현을 찾아 우리말에 맞게 영어로 쓰시오.

1 일찍 일어나는 것은 힘들다.

_____

2 블로그들을 읽는 것은 재미있다.

_____

3 꿈을 갖는 것은 중요하다.

_____

4 매일 일기를 쓰는 것은 좋다.

_____

5 그 표를 구한 것은 행운이었다.

_____

6 헬멧을 쓰는 것은 안전하다.

_____

7 선물을 열어보는 것은 신난다.

_____

lucky interesting safe important hard exciting good

open a present get the ticket wear a helmet get up early have a dream write in a diary read blogs

C 그림을 보고 주어진 표현을 활용하여 건강과 관련된 습관에 대해 쓰시오.

0

It is healthy to jog every morning.

It is unhealthy to sit all day.

- every morning   - all day

1

1) _____

2) _____

- a lot of water   - a lot of Coke

2

1) _____

2) _____

- vegetables
  and fruit
- fast food

WRAP UP

A   그림을 보고 질문에 알맞은 대답을 쓰시오.

1   What is the date today? – _____

2   What day is it today? – _____

3   What time is it now? – _____

4   How is the weather today? – _____

5   Is it bright in the living room? – No, it isn't. _____

B   그림을 보고 주어진 단어와 보기의 표현을 활용하여 발명품의 장점에 대한 문장을 쓰시오.

0	1	2	3

- convenient	- fun	- easy	- possible

clean the floor   protect one's fingers   drink juice

0   It is convenient to use toothpaste with it.

1   _____

2   _____

3   _____

C 다음 우리말에 맞게 영어로 쓰시오.

1
_____

오늘은 흐리고 바람이 분다.

2
_____

사진을 찍는 것은 즐겁다. (fun)

3
_____

내일은 5월 5일이다.

4
_____

혼자서 여행하는 것은 위험하다. (alone)

5
_____

호주는 겨울이다. (Australia)

6
_____

약속을 지키는 것은 중요하다. (promises)

7
_____

여기에서 도서관까지는 500미터이다. (from ~ to …)

8
_____

습관을 바꾸는 것은 어렵다. (hard, habit)

D 다음 우리말에 맞게 영어로 쓰시오.

1

> 1) 어두웠다. Sarah was on her way home. She heard a strange sound. 2) 혼자서 걸어가는 것이 무서웠다.

1) _____

2) _____ (alone)

2

> Peter and I went to the amusement park. We rode exciting rides. 1) 놀이기구들을 타는 것은 즐거웠다. But 2) 비가 오기 시작했다. We went back home.

1) _____ (ride)

2) _____ (begin)

E 주어진 정보를 바탕으로 일기를 쓰시오.

0 August 14th ☀ (exciting, swim at the beach)

It was August 14th.
It was sunny.
It was *exciting to swim at the beach*.

1 December 23rd ❄ (fun, have a snowball fight)

1) _____
2) _____
3) _____

2 July 12th ☔ (boring, stay at home)

1) _____
2) _____
3) _____

F 외출하려는 동생에게 현재 날씨와 꼭 챙겨야 할 물품에 대해 알려 주려고 한다. 그림을 보고 주어진 어구를 활용하여 메시지를 쓰시오.

0
- sunny / hat

1
- cold / thick coat

2
- rainy / umbrella

0 It is sunny outside. It is necessary to wear a hat.

1 _____

2 _____

LESSON 11
형용사와 부사

marry	wisely	perfect	violinist
princess	suddenly	score	hang out with
sweet	fail	audition	ring
scary	bark	shake	fall down
scarf	loudly	dash	slippery
popular	lose	surprisingly	hurt
fat	heavily	win	comfortable
lucky	shout	race	stylish
blouse	enter	woods	platform
spend	carefully	scared	hold

UNIT1 형용사의 역할과 위치

*My master married a **beautiful** princess.*
*They are **happy**. I am **happy**, too.*

★ 형용사는 사물의 성질이나 상태를 나타낼 때 쓴다.

1 명사를 수식하는 경우, 그 앞에 쓴다.

I want a **big** *desk*.　　　　My brother likes **sweet** *candy*.

2 주어나 목적어를 보충 설명하는 경우, 동사나 목적어 뒤에 쓴다.

Dogs are **smart**.　　　　*The potato pizza* is **delicious**.
The book made *her* **famous**.　　I found *the sitcom* **fun**.

A　괄호 안의 단어를 배열하여 올바른 문장으로 다시 쓰시오.

1　나는 새 스마트폰을 샀다. (bought, I, smartphone, a, new)

　　　--

2　그 공포 영화는 무서웠다. (movie, scary, the, was, horror)

　　　--

3　나는 그 시험이 어렵다는 것을 알았다. (difficult, found, I, the, test)

　　　--

4　우리는 작은 호텔에 머물렀다. (small, in, a, stayed, we, hotel)

　　　--

5　이 박스들은 무겁다. (heavy, are, boxes, these)

　　　--

6　이 목도리는 당신을 따뜻하게 유지해 줄 것입니다. (keep, warm, you, this, will, scarf)

　　　--

7　그는 나에게 재미있는 이야기를 말해주었다. (told, an, me, interesting, he, story)

　　　--

8　그 소식은 그를 행복하게 해주었다. (made, the, him, news, happy)

　　　--

9　내 남동생은 학교에서 인기가 많다. (my, popular, is, brother, at school)

　　　--

B   보기에서 알맞은 단어를 찾아 우리말에 맞게 영어로 쓰시오.

1   나는 신선한 토마토를 샀다.

2   그 수학 시험은 쉬웠다.

3   그 영화는 나를 슬프게 했다.

4   이 양파 수프는 달다.

5   그들은 큰 집에 산다.

6   좋은 음식은 너를 건강하게 유지해준다.

7   7은 행운의 숫자이다.

| sweet |
| easy |
| sad |
| healthy |
| fresh |
| lucky |
| big |

C   그림을 보고 각 보기에서 알맞은 표현을 찾아 은행 강도를 묘사하는 문장을 쓰시오.

| fat |
| tall |

| blouse |
| jacket |
| skirt |
| pants |

0   He was slim. He wore a yellow shirt and green pants.

1   1)

2)

2   1)

2)

UNIT 2 부사의 역할과 위치

*Sadly, my master can make **only** one wish.*

★ 부사는 형용사, 부사, 동사 또는 문장 전체를 수식하며, 시간, 방법, 정도 등의 의미를 좀 더 구체적으로 표현한다.

1 형용사나 부사를 수식하는 경우, 그 앞에 쓴다.
The English test was **really** *difficult.*   Kevin speaks Korean **very** *well.*

2 동사를 수식하는 경우, 보통 동사 뒤에 쓰나 목적어가 있으면 그 뒤에 쓴다.
Koalas *move* **slowly.**   Mike *spends* his money **wisely.**

3 문장 전체를 수식하는 경우, 보통 문장 처음에 쓴다.
Suddenly, *the snow stopped.*   **Sadly**, *James failed the test.*

A 주어진 부사를 알맞은 곳에 넣어 문장을 다시 쓰시오.

1 The dog barks loudly. (too)

_____

2 My brother is tall. (very)

_____

3 We lost the game. (sadly)

_____

4 Tom studied math hard. (really)

_____

5 It rained this morning. (heavily)

_____

6 I found my cell phone. (luckily)

_____

7 The birds fly in the sky. (high)

_____

8 The fruit was fresh. (really)

_____

> *Tips for Writing*
>
> 문장 앞에 부사가 오는 경우 부사 바로 뒤에 쉼표(,)를 사용하기도 한다.

B 보기에서 알맞은 단어를 찾아 우리말에 맞게 영어로 쓰시오.

1 나의 아빠는 집에 일찍 오셨다.

_____

2 갑자기 그 소녀는 소리쳤다.

_____

3 그 케이크는 정말 달았다.

_____

4 나는 그 가게를 쉽게 찾았다.

_____

5 솔직히 나는 너의 공책을 잃어버렸다.

_____

6 나는 어제 매우 피곤했다.

_____

7 Dave는 교실에 조용히 들어왔다.

_____

| suddenly |
| really |
| early |
| honestly |
| very |
| easily |
| quietly |

C 주어진 표현과 보기의 단어를 활용하여 어제 있었던 일에 대해 쓰시오.

| sadly | fast | badly | surprisingly |

0

- solve the questions
- get a perfect score

I took a test yesterday.

I solved the questions carefully.

Luckily, I got a perfect score.

1

- shake
- fail the audition

I had an audition yesterday.

1) _____

2) _____

2

- run
- win the race

I ran a 100-meter dash yesterday.

1) _____

2) _____

WRAP UP

A   그림을 보고 보기에서 알맞은 단어를 찾아 헨젤과 그레텔의 이야기를 완성하시오.

0   　1   　2   　3

scared　　delicious　　hungry

0   Hansel and Gretel walked and walked in the woods.

They were very tired.

1   They didn't eat any food all day.

_____

2   They saw a cookie house and ate it.

_____

3   Suddenly, the witch came.

_____

B   다음 질문에 알맞은 대답을 쓰시오.

0   Is Youngmi a slow eater?

Yes, she is. *She is a slow eater. She eats slowly.*

1   Is Mary a careful driver?

Yes, she is. _____

2   Is Bolt a fast runner?

Yes, he is. _____

3   Is Emily a good violinist?

Yes, she is. _____

4   Is Jaeseok a hard worker?

Yes, he is. _____

C 다음 우리말에 맞게 영어로 쓰시오.

1

우리는 거리를 깨끗이 유지해야 한다. (street)

2

그녀는 도서관에서 조용히 이야기했다.

3

이 지갑은 저렴하고 검정색이다. (wallet)

4

John은 그 수학 문제를 빨리 풀었다.

5

나는 그 식당에서 유명한 가수를 보았다. (restaurant)

6

책을 읽는 것은 나를 졸리게 한다. (sleepy)

7

슬프게도 Joan은 다음 달에 서울로 이사 갈 것이다. (move)

D 다음 우리말에 맞게 영어로 쓰시오.

1

> Jerry had an important exam the next day. 1) 그는 그의 방에서 열심히 공부하고 있었다. 2) 갑자기 그의 휴대전화가 울렸다. His friend wanted to hang out with him. But he didn't go. He kept studying.

1) _____

2) _____ (ring)

2

> It snowed very heavily this morning. 1) 도로는 매우 미끄러웠다. 2) 나는 아주 조심해서 걸었다. But I fell down. It really hurt.

1) _____ (slippery)

2) _____

E 주어진 정보를 바탕으로 가게를 홍보하는 글을 쓰시오.

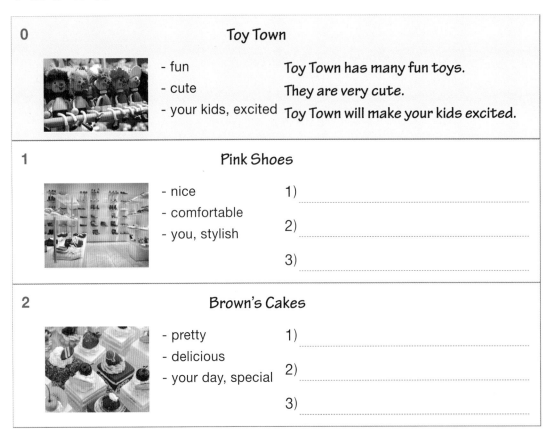

0	Toy Town	
	- fun	Toy Town has many fun toys.
	- cute	They are very cute.
	- your kids, excited	Toy Town will make your kids excited.

1	Pink Shoes	
	- nice	1) ....
	- comfortable	2) ....
	- you, stylish	3) ....

2	Brown's Cakes	
	- pretty	1) ....
	- delicious	2) ....
	- your day, special	3) ....

F 다음 그림을 보고, 보기에서 알맞은 단어를 찾아 지하철 승강장에 있는 등장인물들의 행동을 묘사한 문장을 쓰시오.

| beautiful |
| loudly |
| heavy |

There are some people on the subway platform.

1   An old lady ....

2   A girl ....

3   A tall man ....

LESSON 12

비교

before	island	mountain	cross
rice	chapter	ocean	finish line
silk	museum	diamond	waterfall
soft	building	hard	lake
cotton	town	iron	deep
watermelon	busy	handsome	product
air conditioner	diligent	bridge	offline
fan	country	turtle	convenient
set	light	race	review
expensive	world	give up	shopping hours

UNIT 1 비교급

*My master is **happier than** before. I am **happier than** him.*

★ '~보다 더 …한[하게]'라는 의미로 두 대상을 비교할 때 〈비교급 + than〉을 쓴다.
Today is **colder than** yesterday.
Minhee speaks English **better than** Junwoo.
The movie is **more interesting than** the book.

A 괄호 안의 단어를 배열하여 올바른 문장으로 다시 쓰시오.

1 이번 주가 지난주보다 더 따뜻하다. (warmer, this week, is, last week, than)

    ....

2 Ron은 Anne보다 더 열심히 공부했다. (Anne, harder, studied, Ron, than)

    ....

3 미나는 빵보다 밥을 더 좋아한다. (more, bread, Mina, rice, likes, than)

    ....

4 Joan은 그녀의 엄마보다 더 키가 크다. (than, taller, her mother, is, Joan)

    ....

5 내 형의 방은 내 것보다 더 크다. (mine, bigger, my brother's room, than, is)

    ....

6 건강은 돈보다 더 중요하다. (money, is, than, important, health, more)

    ....

7 이 지갑은 저것보다 더 저렴하다. (that one, than, cheaper, this wallet, is)

    ....

8 실크는 면보다 더 부드럽다. (softer, cotton, is, silk, than)

    ....

9 Lucy의 개는 Lucy보다 더 일찍 일어난다.
   (wakes up, Lucy, than, Lucy's dog, earlier)

    ....

B 그림을 보고 주어진 표현과 보기의 단어를 활용하여 두 대상을 비교하는 문장을 쓰시오.

0	1	2	3
- a soccer ball - a golf ball	- the Eiffel Tower - the 63 Building	- the KTX - the bus	- a watermelon - an orange

tall   heavy   fast

0 A soccer ball is bigger than a golf ball.

1 _____

2 _____

3 _____

C 주어진 단어를 활용하여 더 좋아하는 것에 대해 설명하는 문장을 쓰시오.

0
- comic books
- newspapers
- exciting

Kate likes comic books more than newspapers .

Comic books are more exciting than newspapers.

1
- emails
- letters
- fast

1) John _____ .

2) _____

2
- air conditioners
- fans
- cool

1) Chris _____ .

2) _____

UNIT 2 최상급

★ '가장 ~한'의 의미로 세 가지 이상을 비교하여 정도가 가장 높은 것을 표현할 때
⟨the + 최상급⟩을 쓴다.

Ron is **the tallest** boy in my class.
Football is **the most popular** sport in England.
February is **the shortest** of the twelve months.

> **note**
> 최상급의 비교 범위를 나타낼 때
> ⟨in + 장소 · 범위를 나타내는
> 단수명사⟩나 ⟨of + 비교 대상이
> 되는 명사⟩를 쓴다.

A 괄호 안의 표현을 활용하여 우리말에 맞게 영어로 쓰시오.

0 이곳이 이 호텔에서 가장 큰 방이다. (this, a large room, in this hotel)

This is the largest room in this hotel.

1 이것은 이 가게에서 가장 비싼 차이다. (this, an expensive car, in this shop)

_____

2 제주도는 한국에서 가장 큰 섬이다. (Jejudo, a large island, in Korea)

_____

3 오늘은 8월 중에서 가장 더운 날이다. (today, a hot day, in August)

_____

4 그것은 이 책에서 가장 어려운 단원이다. (it, a difficult chapter, in this book)

_____

5 Justin은 나의 반에서 가장 인기 있는 소년이다.
(Justin, a popular boy, in my class)

_____

6 주영은 세 명 중 가장 빨리 달리는 선수이다.
(Juyoung, a fast runner, of the three)

_____

7 루브르는 세계에서 가장 큰 박물관이다.
(the Louvre, a big museum, in the world)

_____

B 각 보기에서 알맞은 표현을 찾아 우리말에 맞게 영어로 쓰시오.

1 서울은 한국에서 가장 큰 도시이다.
_____

2 이 교회는 이 마을에서 가장 오래된 건물이다.
_____

3 그 팬더는 이 동물원에서 가장 인기 있는 동물이다.
_____

4 화요일은 일주일 중에 가장 바쁜 날이다.
_____

5 이 장난감이 모든 것 중에 가장 싸다.
_____

6 Tom은 우리 반에서 가장 부지런한 학생이다.
_____

7 Mark는 우리나라에서 가장 부유한 남자이다.
_____

old
diligent
busy
rich
cheap
big
popular

this zoo
one's country
this town
all
the week
Korea
one's class

C 표에 주어진 정보를 바탕으로 세 육상 선수들에 대한 문장을 쓰시오.

Name	James	Eric	Andrew
Weight	63 kg	61 kg	65 kg
Height	168 cm	173 cm	171 cm
Speed Record	11 sec	12 sec	13 sec

0 **James** is the shortest runner of the three _____ . <height>

He is the fastest runner of the three. _____ <speed record>

1 1) Eric _____ . <weight>

2) _____ <height>

2 1) Andrew _____ . <weight>

2) _____ <speed record>

WRAP UP

A 주어진 정보를 보고 괄호 안의 단어를 활용하여 스마트폰과 태블릿 PC를 비교하는 문장을 쓰시오.

Smartphone		Tablet PC	
	4.8 inches		9 inches
	140 g		600 g
	$400		$700

0 (small / large)

The smartphone is smaller than the tablet PC.

The tablet PC is larger than the smartphone.

1 (light / heavy)

1) ....

2) ....

2 (cheap / expensive)

1) ....

2) ....

B 괄호 안의 단어를 활용하여 다음과 같이 세계 최고 기록을 가진 것에 대한 문장을 쓰시오.

0 (Vatican City, small, country)

Vatican City is the smallest country in the world.

1 (Mt. Everest, high, mountain)

....

2 (the Nile River, long, river)

....

3 (the Pacific Ocean, wide, ocean)

....

4 (the cheetah, fast, animal)

....

C 다음 우리말에 맞게 영어로 쓰시오.

1

다이아몬드는 철보다 더 단단하다. (diamonds, hard, iron)

2

러시아는 세계에서 가장 큰 나라이다. (Russia)

3

내 남자친구는 Brad보다 더 잘생겼다. (handsome)

4

인천대교는 한국에서 가장 긴 다리이다. (the Incheon Bridge)

5

Jay는 Grace보다 더 빨리 수영한다.

6

이 카메라가 넷 중에서 가장 비싸다.

7

내 컴퓨터가 너의 것보다 더 오래되었다.

D 다음 우리말에 맞게 영어로 쓰시오.

1

> A turtle and a rabbit ran in a race. 1) 토끼는 거북이보다 더 빨리 달렸다. But the rabbit slept and the turtle didn't give up. Finally, 2) 거북이는 토끼보다 더 일찍 결승선을 넘었다.

1) ....

2) .... (cross, the finish line)

2

> I traveled in Paris, Rome and Prague last summer. I liked Prague. 1) 프라하는 세 곳 중 가장 아름다운 도시였다. I didn't like Rome. 2) 로마는 세 곳 중 가장 더운 도시였다.

1) ....

2) ....

E 주어진 정보를 바탕으로 다음과 같이 비교하는 글을 쓰시오.

0	World Record Waterfalls - high	1st-Angel Falls(3,212 feet) 2nd-Tugela Falls(3,110 feet) Angel Falls is higher than Tugela Falls. Angel Falls is the highest waterfall in the world.
1	World Record Beaches - long	1st-Cox's Bazar Beach(150 miles) 2nd-Ninety Mile Beach(90 miles) 1) _____ 2) _____
2	World Record Lakes - deep	1st-Lake Baikal(1,637 meters) 2nd-Lake Tanganyika(1,470 meters) 1) _____ 2) _____

F 보기에서 온라인 상점의 장점에 해당하는 표현을 두 개 골라 그 장점에 대한 문장을 오프라인 상점과 비교하여 쓰시오.

convenient	cheap	many reviews	long shopping hours

0 Online shops have more products than offline shops.

1 _____

2 _____

SECTION 3
PATTERNS FOR WRITING

Useful Patterns *for Writing 1*

★ one's favorite ~ is …: −가 가장 좋아하는 ~는 …이다
  My favorite sport **is** soccer.

★ hate + 목적어: ~을 싫어한다
  I **hate** summer.

1 내가 가장 좋아하는 색은 파란색이다.

2 Alex는 테니스를 싫어한다.

3 Kate가 가장 좋아하는 음식은 피자다.

4 내 남동생은 뜨거운 우유를 싫어한다.

5 Anne이 가장 좋아하는 도시는 로마이다. (Rome)

6 그는 수학을 싫어한다. (math)

7 Nick이 가장 좋아하는 과목은 영어다.

8 Emma는 공포영화를 싫어한다. (horror movies)

9 그녀가 가장 좋아하는 달은 4월이다.

10 나는 월요일 아침을 싫어한다.

Useful Patterns *for Writing 2*

★ keep + 목적어 + 형용사: ~을 …하도록 유지하다
My mother **keeps vegetables fresh.**

★ be tired of: ~이 싫증나다[지겹다]
I **am tired of** my job.

1 Luke는 그의 방을 깨끗하게 유지한다.

2 John은 그의 오래된 차가 싫증난다.

3 나의 누나는 그 창문을 열어 놓는다.

4 나의 할머니는 이 추운 날씨를 지겨워하신다.

5 그들은 그 계획을 비밀로 유지한다. (secret)

6 나는 내 검정 머리가 지겹다.

7 큰 창문들이 그 집을 밝게 유지해준다. (bright)

8 Adam은 그 일을 지겨워한다. (work)

9 Emily는 그녀의 손톱들을 짧게 유지한다. (nail)

10 Carrie는 바쁜 도시 생활에 싫증 나 한다. (city life)

Useful Patterns for Writing 3

★ don't like ~: ~을 좋아하지 않는다
I don't like chocolate cakes.

★ enjoy v-ing: ~하는 것을 즐긴다
My brother **enjoys drinking** coffee.

1   Julie는 이탈리아 음식을 좋아하지 않는다. (Italian)

2   나는 TV 보는 것을 즐긴다.

3   Sophia는 닭고기를 좋아하지 않는다.

4   나의 아빠는 요리하는 것을 즐기신다.

5   나는 그녀의 새 책을 좋아하지 않는다.

6   내 친구들은 야구하는 것을 즐긴다.

7   Henry는 록음악을 좋아하지 않는다. (rock music)

8   우리는 아이스크림 먹는 것을 즐긴다.

9   Terry는 축구를 좋아하지 않는다.

10   나의 가족은 기차로 여행하는 것을 즐긴다.

Useful Patterns *for Writing 4*

★ What / How about v-ing ~?: ~하는 게 어때요?
What about playing basketball?

★ How long / much / often ~?: 얼마나 오래[긴]/얼마나 많이/얼마나 자주 ~ 하나요[인가요]?
How often do you drink water?

1　함께 공부하는 게 어떠니? (together)

2　당신의 여름 휴가는 얼마나 긴가요?

3　이 시계를 사는 게 어떠니?

4　너는 나를 얼마나 사랑하니?

5　내일 외식하는 게 어떠니? (eat out)

6　Amy는 얼마나 자주 피아노를 치니?

7　TV로 올림픽 경기를 보는 게 어떠니? (the Olympic games)

8　너는 와인에 대해서 얼마나 아니? (wine)

9　지금 집에 가는 게 어떠니?

10　만리장성은 얼마나 기니? (the Great Wall of China)

Useful Patterns for Writing 5

★ I am sorry but ~: 죄송하지만 ~
  I am sorry but I don't like this hat.

★ Thank you for v-ing: ~해주셔서 감사합니다
  Thank you for helping me.

1 죄송하지만 제가 지금 바빠요.

_____

2 저에게 전화해 주셔서 감사해요.

_____

3 죄송하지만 저는 그를 몰라요.

_____

4 저를 기다려 주셔서 감사해요. (wait for)

_____

5 죄송하지만 저는 당신을 믿지 않아요. (believe)

_____

6 저희 가게를 방문해 주셔서 감사합니다.

_____

7 죄송하지만 저는 피자를 싫어해요.

_____

8 저를 초대해주셔서 감사합니다. (invite)

_____

9 죄송하지만 전 당신에게 동의하지 않아요. (agree with)

_____

10 저에게 선물을 보내주셔서 감사합니다.

_____

Useful Patterns *for Writing* 6

★ Why don't you ~?: ~하는 게 어때요?
Why don't you sit here?

★ Would you ~?: ~해 주시겠어요?
Would you close the door?

1   노트북 컴퓨터를 사는 게 어때요? (laptop)

2   저를 도와주시겠어요?

3   그녀에게 물어보는 게 어때요?

4   제게 샌드위치 하나를 사다 주시겠어요? (sandwich)

5   버스를 타는 게 어때요? (take a bus)

6   제게 당신의 펜을 빌려주시겠어요? (lend)

7   지금 저녁을 먹는 게 어때요?

8   당신의 전화번호를 제게 말해주시겠어요?

9   나와 스케이트장에 가는 게 어때요? (ice rink)

10   한국의 문화를 설명해 주시겠어요?

Useful Patterns *for Writing* 7

★ come to-v: ~하러 오다
Many people **came to watch** the play.

★ prove to-v: ~로 판명되다
The information **proved to be** wrong.

1   나의 가족은 새 집을 보러 왔다.

    ....

2   그 시험은 어려운 것으로 판명되었다.

    ....

3   Carter는 나에게 선물을 주러 왔다.

    ....

4   그 남자는 Jay의 삼촌으로 판명되었다.

    ....

5   Grace는 나와 함께 숙제를 하러 왔다.

    ....

6   그 소식은 사실로 판명되었다.

    ....

7   우리는 Ron의 집을 방문하러 왔다.

    ....

8   그 도둑은 Eric으로 판명되었다. (thief)

    ....

9   Emily는 작별 인사를 하러 왔다. (say goodbye)

    ....

10 그의 콘서트는 성공적이라고 판명되었다. (successful)

    ....

Useful Patterns *for Writing* 8

★ be afraid + 주어 + can't~: ~하지 못할 것 같다
I am afraid I can't finish the report.

★ be busy v-ing: ~하느라 바쁘다
I am busy packing.

1 나는 그 질문들에 대답하지 못할 것 같네요.

2 나는 영어 시험을 준비하느라 바쁘다. (prepare for)

3 나는 당신의 이름을 기억하지 못할 것 같네요.

4 Linda는 피아노 연습을 하느라 바쁘다. (practice)

5 나는 당신의 차를 수리하지 못할 것 같네요. (fix)

6 그녀는 그녀의 집을 청소하느라 바쁘다.

7 나는 당신을 내일 만나지 못할 것 같네요.

8 James는 컴퓨터 게임을 하느라 바쁘다.

9 나는 그 비밀번호를 기억하지 못할 것 같네요. (password)

10 그들은 수학을 공부하느라 바쁘다.

Useful Patterns *for Writing* 9

★ feel like v-ing: ~하고 싶다
  I **feel like washing** my hands.

★ Do you mind v-ing?: ~해주시겠습니까?
  Do you mind lending me your baseball bat?

1 Eva는 오늘 쇼핑하러 가고 싶어한다.

   ....

2 당신의 카메라를 가져와 주시겠습니까?

   ....

3 나는 지금 외출하고 싶다. (go out)

   ....

4 제 사진을 찍어주시겠습니까? (take a picture of)

   ....

5 Ben은 샌드위치를 먹고 싶어한다.

   ....

6 당신의 모자를 벗어주시겠습니까? (take off)

   ....

7 Justin은 이 책을 읽고 싶어한다.

   ....

8 문을 열어주시겠습니까?

   ....

9 나는 당신과 춤을 추고 싶습니다.

   ....

10 히터를 꺼주시겠습니까? (turn off)

   ....

Useful Patterns *for Writing 10*

★ It is worth v-ing: ~할 가치가 있다
It is worth helping poor people.

★ hope to-v ~: ~하길 바라다
I **hope to visit** New York again.

1 영어는 배울만한 가치가 있다.

2 Karen은 프랑스에서 살기를 바란다.

3 그 영화는 볼만한 가치가 있다.

4 우리는 당신을 곧 만나길 바란다.

5 그 식당에서 저녁을 먹을만한 가치가 있다.

6 나는 내 개를 찾길 바란다.

7 부모님의 충고는 들을 가치가 있다. (parents' advice)

8 Betty는 Maroon 5 콘서트에 가길 바란다.

9 아이들을 가르치는 것은 가치가 있다.

10 Dana는 여배우가 되기를 희망한다. (actress)

Useful Patterns for Writing 11

★ be (pretty) good at v-ing ~: ~을 (꽤) 잘한다
  I am pretty good at cooking.

★ be glad / sad / happy to-v ~: ~해서 기쁘다 / 슬프다 / 행복하다
  I am glad to be with you.

1 Kelly는 노래를 잘한다.

2 Erica는 이 나라를 떠나게 되어 슬퍼한다.

3 Tony는 글쓰기를 꽤 잘했다.

4 나는 그 소식을 들어 행복하다.

5 그녀는 일본어로 말하는 것을 꽤 잘한다.

6 Joe는 그 호텔에 머물게 되어 기뻤다. (stay)

7 나의 아빠는 낚시를 잘하신다.

8 Carol은 그녀의 휴대전화를 잃어버려서 슬프다. (lose)

9 나는 그림을 잘 그린다.

10 우리는 휴가를 갖게 되어 행복하다. (vacation)

Useful Patterns *for Writing* 12

★ prefer A to B: B보다 A를 더 좋아하다
  I **prefer meat to fish.**

★ 비교급 + and + 비교급: 점점 더 ~한
  It is getting **hotter and hotter.**

1   Julia는 여름보다 봄을 더 좋아한다.

2   점점 더 어두워지고 있다.

3   나는 빨간색보다 파란색을 더 좋아한다.

4   이 나무는 점점 더 크게 자란다. (tall)

5   내 여동생은 토마토 주스보다 오렌지 주스를 더 좋아한다.

6   내 삶은 점점 더 좋아지고 있다.

7   Andrew는 록 음악보다 힙합을 더 좋아한다. (rock music)

8   인터넷이 점점 더 빨라지고 있다. (the Internet)

9   젊은 사람들은 골프보다 테니스를 더 좋아한다.

10 날씨가 점점 더 추워지고 있다.

WORD LIST

LESSON 1

classmate 반 친구
history 역사
difficult 어려운
police officer 경찰관
comic book 만화책

—

country 나라
smart 똑똑한
pianist 피아니스트
hungry 배고픈
twin 쌍둥이

—

diligent 부지런한
player 선수
classroom 교실
neighbor 이웃
beautiful 아름다운

—

writer 작가
baker 제빵사
nurse 간호사
magic 마법의
power 힘

—

ride 타다
bike 자전거
bake (음식을) 굽다
magazine 잡지
teach 가르치다

—

math 수학
drama 드라마
learn 배우다
yoga 요가
collect 수집하다

—

school uniform 교복
check 확인하다
download 다운로드 하다
hamster 햄스터
vegetable 야채

—

meat 고기
thin 마른
businessman 회사원

heavy 육중한
famous 유명한

—

slim 날씬한
basketball 농구
elementary school 초등학교
treat 치료하다
sick 아픈

—

cook 요리사; 요리하다
delicious 맛있는
sportsman 운동선수
actress 여배우
science 과학

—

class 수업
scary 무서운
friendly 다정한
same 같은
clothes 옷

—

similar 비슷한
glasses 안경
place 장소
visit 방문하다
fast 빠른

—

sushi 초밥
fresh 신선한
slow 느린

LESSON 2

neckache 목의 통증
secret 비밀
funny 우스운
joke 농담
parent 부모

—

question 질문
lend 빌려주다
gift 선물
bring 가져오다
story 이야기

—

homework 숙제

skin 피부
special 특별한
lie 거짓말
keep 유지하다

—

novel 소설
genius 천재
boring 지루한
convenient 편리한
dishwasher 식기 세척기

—

dish 그릇
wizard 마법사
regular 규칙적인
exercise 운동
healthy 건강한

—

interesting 재미있는
excited 흥분한
tired 피곤한
score 점수
blanket 담요

—

thirsty 목이 마른
textbook 교과서
refrigerator 냉장고
microwave 전자레인지
air cleaner 공기 청정기

—

air conditioner 에어컨
cousin 사촌
worry 고민
during ~동안
bookworm 독서광

—

busy 바쁜

LESSON 3

----

comfortable 편안한
shy 수줍어하는
save 절약하다
breakfast 아침 식사
rub 문지르다

—

quiet 조용한

together 함께
beach 해변
turn off (전기 등을) 끄다
eat out 외식하다

—

noise 소음
correct 수정하다
wrong 틀린
stomachache 복통
take medicine 약을 복용하다

—

walk 걷다
mask 마스크
touch 만지다
dry 말리다
fight 싸우다

—

waste 낭비하다
work 작동하다
onion 양파
map 지도

LESSON 4

----

master 주인
designer 디자이너
part-time job 아르바이트
sitcom 시트콤
exciting 흥미진진한

—

too 너무
address 주소
wish 소망
feel 느끼다
come from ~ 출신이다

—

favorite 가장 좋아하는
actor 배우
restroom 화장실
hall 복도
station 역

—

job 직업
festival 축제
playground 운동장
title 제목

age 나이

—

grandparents 조부모
well 잘
close 친한
vacation 방학
museum 박물관

—

holiday 휴일
modern 현대의
gallery 미술관

LESSON 5

plate 그릇
frog 개구리
parking lot 주차장
bank 은행
weekend 주말

—

seesaw 시소
swing 그네
slide 미끄럼틀
cave 동굴
bus stop 버스정류장

—

wallet 지갑
zoo 동물원
bottle 병
leave 떠나다
pet 애완동물

—

iguana 이구아나
bat 방망이
pencil case 필통
put 두다
paper 종이

—

wise 현명한
lake 호수
active 활동적인
on stage 무대에
theater 극장

LESSON 6

call 전화하다
surf the Internet 인터넷을 검색하다
Earth 지구
round 둥근
homeroom teacher 담임 교사

—

take a test 시험을 보다
model plane 모형 비행기
horror 공포
scream 비명을 지르다
a lot 많이

—

comedy 코미디
laugh 웃다
romantic 로맨틱
fantastic 환상적인
tomorrow 내일

—

next 다음
early 일찍
move 이사하다
end 끝나다
join 가입하다

—

headache 두통
present 선물
break 고장 내다
travel 여행하다
build (건물을) 짓다

—

ago 전에
trip 여행
seafood 해산물
there 거기에서
activity 활동

—

tour 여행
farm 농장
peak (산의) 봉우리
sunset 저녁 노을
miss 놓치다

LESSON 7

wait for ~를 기다리다
wish 소원
diary 일기
stay 머무르다
in line 일렬로

chat 이야기를 나누다
pool 수영장
update 최근 정보를 덧붙이다
blog (인터넷의) 블로그
sand castle 모래성

lie 눕다
volleyball 배구
gym (학교 등의) 체육관
essay 에세이
take a shower 샤워를 하다

brush 칫솔질을 하다
tooth 이
raincoat 비옷
kid 아이
stage 무대

climb 오르다
fix 고치다
wash dishes 설거지하다
take a walk 산책하다
look for 찾다

sunglasses 선글라스
kick 공을 차다
classroom 교실
slow down (속도)를 줄이다
sweep 쓸다

floor 바닥
move 옮기다
blow up (입으로) 불다
balloon 풍선
smile 미소 짓다

paint 페인트칠하다
wall 벽
cafeteria 카페테리아

animal 동물
giraffe 기린

leaf 잎

LESSON 8

kill 죽이다
skate 스케이트를 타다
backpack 배낭
attend 참석하다
meeting 회의

carry 나르다
alone 혼자서
try on 입어보다
discount 할인
borrow 빌리다

textbook 교과서
cross 횡단하다
street 길
ride 타다; 놀이 기구
apologize 사과하다

spend 쓰다
promise 약속
truth 진실
fasten 매다
seat belt 안전벨트

take (교통수단을) 타다
trip 여행
helmet 헬멧
hiking boots 등산화
kung fu 쿵푸

on time 시간을 어기지 않고
flute 플루트
turn on 켜다
heater 히터
solve (문제 등을) 풀다

dictionary 사전
rule 규칙
area 구역

tube 튜브
palace 궁전

—

view 전망
cheap 싼

LESSON 9

get out of ~에서 나가다
plan 계획
abroad 해외로
decide 결심하다
hope 희망하다

—

goal 목표
golfer 골프 선수
hobby 취미
win (메달을) 따다
take a picture 사진을 찍다

—

keep (동물을) 기르다
enjoy 즐기다
astronaut 우주 비행사
dangerous 위험한
promise 약속하다

—

mind 꺼리다
practice 연습하다
avoid 피하다
give up 포기하다
throw 던지다

—

director 감독
design 디자인하다
action movie 액션 영화
poor 가난한
book report 독후감

—

support 지지하다
prize 상
go on a diet 다이어트하다
lose (살을) 빼다
electric 전자의

—

fondue 퐁듀

LESSON 10

outside (건물 등의)밖, 바깥
spring 봄
cloudy 흐린
dark 어두운
fall 가을

—

bright 밝은, 눈부신
New Year's Day 1월 1일, 새해 첫날
humid 습한
windy 바람이 많이 부는
escape 탈출하다

—

danger 위험
necessary 필요한
honest 정직한
important 중요한
impossible 불가능한

—

find 찾다, 발견하다
hard 어려운
machine 기계
lucky 행운의
jog 조깅하다

—

unhealthy 건강에 해로운
all day 하루 종일
fruit 과일
convenient 편리한, 간편한
toothpaste 치약

—

floor 바닥
possible 가능한
protect 보호하다
finger 손가락
from ~ to ... ~부터 …까지

—

change 바꾸다
on one's way home 집에 돌아오는 도중에
strange 이상한
amusement park 놀이공원
begin 시작하다

—

snowball fight 눈싸움
boring 지겨운
thick 두꺼운

coat 외투, 코트

platform 승강장
hold 들고 있다

LESSON 11

marry ~와 결혼하다
princess 공주
sweet 달콤한
scarf 스카프, 목도리
warm 따뜻한
—

popular 인기 있는
pants 바지
blouse 블라우스
really 정말로, 아주
slowly 느리게, 천천히
—

suddenly 갑자기
sadly 애석하게도, 불행히
fail 낙제하다
bark (개가) 짖다
loudly 큰소리로, 소란하게
—

luckily 운 좋게
shout 외치다
easily 쉽게
enter 들어가다[오다]
quietly 조용하게
—

carefully 주의하여
audition 오디션
shake 떨다
badly 심하게
dash 단거리 경주
—

surprisingly 놀랍게도
woods 숲
witch 마녀
violinist 바이올린 연주자
hang out with 함께 시간을 보내다
—

ring 울리다
fall down 넘어지다
hurt 아프다
slippery 미끄러운
stylish 유행을 따른
—

LESSON 12

before 전에
rice 밥
health 건강
silk 비단, 실크
soft 부드러운
—

cotton 면
watermelon 수박
fan 선풍기
set (~한 상태에 있게) 하다
island 섬
—

chapter (책의) 장, 단원
church 교회
town 마을
diligent 근면한, 성실한
light 가벼운
—

ocean 대양, 바다
diamond 다이아몬드
hard 단단한
iron 철, 쇠
bridge 다리
—

turtle 거북이
give up 포기하다
finish line 결승선
waterfall 폭포
deep 깊은
—

online shop 온라인 상점
product 상품
offline shop 오프라인 상점
review 평가
shopping hours 영업시간

지은이

NE능률 영어교육연구소

NE능률 영어교육연구소는 혁신적이며 효율적인 영어 교재를 개발하고
영어 학습의 질을 한 단계 높이고자 노력하는 NE능률의 연구조직입니다.

Writing Builder 1

펴 낸 이	주민홍
펴 낸 곳	서울특별시 마포구 월드컵북로 396(상암동) 누리꿈스퀘어 비즈니스타워 10층
	(주)NE능률 (우편번호 03925)
펴 낸 날	2013년 1월 10일 초판 제1쇄 발행
	2024년 3월 15일 제21쇄
전　　화	02 2014 7114
팩　　스	02 3142 0356
홈 페 이 지	www.neungyule.com
등 록 번 호	제 1-68호
I S B N	978-89-6694-538-2 53740
정　　가	10,000원

NE 능률

고객센터

교재 내용 문의 : contact.nebooks.co.kr (별도의 가입 절차 없이 작성 가능)
제품 구매, 교환, 불량, 반품 문의 : 02-2014-7114
☎ 전화문의는 본사 업무시간 중에만 가능합니다.

WRITING BUILDER

정답

1

SECTION 1
SENTENCE STRUCTURE

LESSON 1
문장의 형식 I

UNIT 1

pp.10~11

A

1 Her name is Tiffany.
2 My room is small.
3 Mark and I are classmates.
4 History is difficult.
5 My father is a police officer.
6 The comic books are interesting.
7 China is a big country.
8 My cat is smart.
9 I am a pianist.

B

1 I am hungry.
2 My brothers are twins.
3 Jason is diligent.
4 He is a soccer player.
5 Our classroom is clean.
6 Tom and Amy are neighbors.
7 Her eyes are beautiful.
8 His dog is big.

C

1 1) His name is Paul.
   2) He is fifty years old.
   3) He is a baker.
2 1) Her name is Eva.
   2) She is twenty years old.
   3) She is a nurse.

UNIT 2

pp.12~13

A

1 I ride a bike.
2 Travis bakes bread.
3 I want a bacon sandwich.
4 Nick hates cheesecake.
5 Eddy has many baseball caps.

6 Susan reads a fashion magazine.
7 My father teaches math.
8 Stella has long hair.
9 Sujeong and Minsu like American dramas.

B

1 Our teacher loves us.
2 I know his sister.
3 Grace learns yoga.
4 Chris collects robots.
5 We wear school uniforms.
6 Max and Sue read many books.
7 I check my email every day.
8 We download music files.

C

1 1) likes soccer
   2) He hates baseball.
2 1) likes vegetables
   2) She hates meat.

WRAP UP

pp. 14~16

A

1 is a businessman, He is heavy.
2 is a famous writer, She is slim.
3 is a basketball player, He is tall.
4 is an elementary school student, She is short.

B

1 He cooks delicious food.
2 She drives a big bus.
3 He plays soccer.
4 She teaches English.

C

1 Jessy is an actress.
2 I need a new cell phone.
3 I speak Korean.
4 My science class is interesting.
5 Joey and Sally like scary movies.
6 Her name is Jane.
7 My neighbors are friendly.
8 I know Andy's email address.

D

1 1) They are similar.
   2) They wear the same glasses.
2 1) Gyeongju is a small city.
   2) Many people visit the city.

E

1 1) Haru has sushi.
  2) Sushi is fresh.
  3) The service is kind.
2 1) Italiano has cheese pizza.
  2) Cheese pizza is bad.
  3) The service is slow.

F

1 My name is Yuna.
2 I am fourteen years old.
3 I like movies.

LESSON 2
문장의 형식 Ⅱ

UNIT 1
pp. 18~19

A

1 Jihee tells me funny jokes.
2 Lisa makes her dad a cake.
3 Ben asks his parents questions.
4 Our mother buys us pizza.
5 A clock shows us the time.
6 My dog gives me a kiss.
7 Minsu lends me his eraser.
8 Cathy writes her grandmother a letter.

B

1 My grandparents buy me gifts.
2 Susan sends her friends birthday cards.
3 I ask Rebecca some questions.
4 My sister lends me her clothes.
5 Waiters bring us food.
6 My grandmother tells me stories.
7 I make my brother dinner.

C

1 1) teaches us science
  2) He asks us many questions.
2 1) teaches us Chinese
  2) She shows us some pictures of China.

UNIT 2
pp. 20~21

A

1 This novel makes me sad.
2 We call him a genius.

3 People find the book boring.
4 Computers make life convenient.
5 Dishwashers make dishes clean.
6 We call Harry Potter a wizard.
7 The alarm keeps your house safe.
8 Regular exercise keeps people healthy.

B

1 These boots keep my feet warm.
2 This picture makes me hungry.
3 People call Daniel a prince.
4 Vegetables keep us healthy.
5 People find the movie interesting.
6 My parents call my sister a baby.
7 We keep our classroom clean.

C

1 1) High test scores make me happy.
  2) Low test scores make me sad.
2 1) Nice people make me glad.
  2) Bad people make me angry.

WRAP UP
pp. 22~24

A

1 I give him water.
2 I lend her my history textbook.
3 I make him a sandwich.
4 I teach him English.

B

1 makes food warm
2 makes[keeps] air clean
3 makes a room bright
4 makes[keeps] a room cool

C

1 Jim keeps his desk clean.
2 Mr. Jang teaches us French.
3 The drama makes me sad.
4 I send my cousins Christmas cards.
5 We call our dog Ron.
6 Lily tells her friends her worries.
7 Curtains keep a room warm.
8 June lends me her books.

D

1 1) He teaches us history.
  2) He tells us interesting stories during class.
2 1) I call him a bookworm.

2) He tells me many stories.

E

1 1) We make you a cake.
   2) We send your girlfriend this cake.
2 1) We make you a flower basket.
   2) We send your parents this flower basket.

F

1 I agree. A dog makes us happy.
   [추가 답안] I agree. A dog makes us excited.
2 I disagree. A dog makes us busy.
   [추가 답안] I disagree. A dog makes us tired.

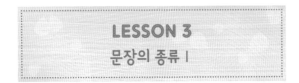

LESSON 3
문장의 종류 I

UNIT 1   pp. 26~27

A

1 Jasmine is not a cook.
2 I do not like rock music.
3 Aiden is not from England.
4 Mike and James are not basketball players.
5 They are not my brothers.
6 Emma does not eat meat.
7 Paul and Judy do not have a lot of homework.
8 Lily does not watch movies.

B

1 I am not sleepy.
2 English is not difficult.
3 Harry does not save energy.
4 I do not like my short hair.
5 Jim and Henry are not my classmates.
6 I do not play the piano.
7 My father does not eat breakfast.

C

1 is not heavy, He does not wear white pants.
2 is not thin, She does not wear a cap.

UNIT 2   pp. 28~29

A

1 Wash your face.
2 Be kind to your friends.
3 Do not enter my room.

4 Let's go to the concert.
5 Turn off your cell phone.
6 Let's order a pizza.
7 Let's not eat out today.
8 Do not be shy.

B

1 Call the police.
2 Do not make noise.
3 Correct the wrong answers.
4 Let's watch a movie.
5 Do not run in the restaurant.
6 Let's eat Korean food.
7 Let's not take a taxi.

C

1 1) Do not play computer games.
   2) Take an online class.
2 1) Do not eat fast food.
   2) Walk to school.

WRAP UP   pp. 30~32

A

1 1) I do not like math.
   2) It is not easy.
2 1) I do not like medicine.
   2) It is not delicious.

B

1 Wash your hands.
2 Drink a lot of water.
3 Do not touch your face.

C

1 Dry your hair.
2 The smartphone is not expensive.
3 Let's not fight.
4 They are not in Seoul.
5 I do not know his phone number.
6 Do not waste your money.
7 Let's start our homework.
8 This computer does not work.

D

1 1) I do not eat carrots.
   2) My sister does not like onions.
2 1) Go to the supermarket.
   2) Do not buy juice.

E

1 1) I do not like the color.
   2) It is not yellow.
2 1) I do not like the size.
   2) It is not small.

F

1 Let's take a map.
2 Let's take a camera.

LESSON 4
문장의 종류 II

UNIT 1

pp. 34~35

A

1 Does your uncle live in Busan?
2 Are Jonghee and Max friends?
3 Do you have a part-time job?
4 Is the sitcom exciting?
5 Does Jennifer go to Seoul Middle School?
6 Is Eric from Australia?
7 Do they go to school by bus?
8 Is this jacket too big for Sam?

B

1 Are you busy now?
2 Does Paul like Korean food?
3 Do you eat breakfast?
4 Is Mr. Anderson a math teacher?
5 Do Alex and Jamie study Chinese?
6 Is this your cell phone?
7 Does he know my address?

C

1 1) Is it white?
   2) Does it climb trees?
2 1) Is it small?
   2) Does it have short ears?

UNIT 2

pp. 36~37

A

1 What do you do in the evening?
2 When is Valentine's Day?
3 How does Sam go to school?
4 Where is my cell phone?
5 When does the hospital open?

6 Who is your favorite actor?
7 What do you want for lunch?
8 Where is the restroom?

B

1 Who is your music teacher?
2 Why do you like summer?
3 Where is the subway station?
4 When does Sean eat[have] dinner?
5 What is Emma's job?
6 How do you study English?
7 When is the school festival?
8 Why are you angry?

C

1 1) What is the title?
   2) When does the play[it] start?
2 1) Who is the singer?
   2) Where is the concert hall?

WRAP UP

pp. 38~40

A

1 Is Andy thirteen years old?
2 Does Amy have a sister?
3 Does Andy like sports?

B

1 Where does Tom go on Sundays?
2 What does Hyunwoo do on Saturdays?
3 When does Jenny go to the cooking class?
4 Who does Suji meet on Saturdays?

C

1 Is the movie scary?
2 Does Emily sing well?
3 How do you make pizza?
4 Who is your close friend?
5 Why do you go to London?
6 Where does your father work?
7 What do you do after school?

D

1 1) Do you like Mexican food?
   2) Do you know Taco Hill?
2 1) How is your new school?
   2) When does your vacation start?

E

1 1) When does the museum close?

5

2) Is it open on holidays?
2 1) Where is the gallery?
   2) Does the gallery open at 8:30 a.m.?

F

1 Where is the party?
2 What do you want for your birthday?

LESSON 5
문장의 확장

UNIT 1

pp. 42~43

A

1 A ball is under the bench.
2 Frogs sleep in winter.
3 Let's meet at the library.
4 My class ends at 4:30.
5 Many cars are in the parking lot.
6 The hospital closes on Sundays.
7 The bank is next to my house.
8 My father plays golf on weekends.
9 My bag is on the desk.

B

1 is by[next to] the bench
2 is on the swing
3 is under the slide

UNIT 2
pp. 43~44

A

1 There is a wallet on the chair.
2 There are two pandas in the zoo.
3 There is a bicycle by[next to] the bench.
4 There is some juice in the bottle.
5 There are 35 students in our class.
6 There is a rabbit under the tree.

B

1 There are two dolls by[next to] the TV.
2 There are some towels in the basket.
3 There is a dog under the chair.

UNIT 3
pp. 44~45

A

1 My dog is cute and smart.

2 Jamie leaves today or tomorrow.
3 I like basketball, but I don't play it.
4 His name is Ming, and he is from China.
5 Mark and Dana speak Korean well.
6 Do you want hot chocolate or juice?
7 I know his face, but I don't know his name.
8 Minji has two sisters and one brother.

B

1 1) Tom and Minju eat chocolate.
   2) Tom eats chocolate cake, but Minju doesn't
      eat it.
2 1) Jiho and Julie like pets.
   2) Jiho likes iguanas, but Julie doesn't like them.

WRAP UP
pp. 46~48

A

1 There are (two) cushions on the bed.
2 There is a bat under the desk.
3 There is a teddy bear by[next to] the bed.

B

1 1) Max has some books and a pencil case.
   2) Peter has some books, but he doesn't have a
      pencil case.
2 1) Olivia brings pizza and Coke.
   2) Sumin brings Coke, but she doesn't bring
      pizza.

C

1 My birthday is in May.
2 James sits by[next to] me.
3 I put my keys on the table.
4 There is milk in the refrigerator. / Milk is in the
   refrigerator.
5 There are many stars in the sky. / Many stars are
   in the sky.
6 I need paper and a pen now.
7 Mary is young, but she is wise.
8 Let's eat[have] pizza or spaghetti.

D

1 1) There is a big lake in the park. / A big lake is
      in the park.
   2) There are many birds in the trees. / Many
      birds are in the trees.
2 1) Jane and Susan are close friends.
   2) Jane is active, but Susan is quiet.

E

1 1) *Marine Boy* is on stage on July 11th.
   2) It starts at 3:00 p.m.
   3) It is in the AM Theater.
2 1) *King Bear* is on stage on May 24th.
   2) It starts at 5:00 p.m.
   3) It is in the Seoul Art Center.

F

1 There is a box under the desk.
2 There are (two) soccer balls in the box.
3 There are (four) books on the desk.

SECTION 2
GRAMMAR FOR WRITING

LESSON 6
시제 I

UNIT 1

pp. 52~53

A

1 I made a sandwich for my parents.
2 His birthday was on Saturday.
3 They went to the mall after school.
4 Mr. Smith was my homeroom teacher.
5 Lisa and I were in the theater.
6 The concert started at 7:00 p.m.
7 There were many people at the station.
8 I took a science test this afternoon.

B

1 visited her grandparents last weekend
2 bought a smartphone last Tuesday
3 made a model plane yesterday

C

1 1) I watched a comedy.
   2) It was funny.
   3) I laughed a lot.
2 1) I watched a romantic movie.
   2) It was sad.
   3) I cried a lot.

UNIT 2

pp. 54~55

A

1 A new bakery will open this month.
2 We will watch movies on Saturday.
3 My family will move to Daejeon next year.
4 I will help you with your homework tomorrow.
5 Jaemin will come to my birthday party next week.
6 This concert will end at ten o'clock.
7 Sujin will take yoga classes next month.
8 We will be high school students next year.

B

1 I will finish the work tomorrow.
2 I will read these books this weekend.
3 Monica will buy a red car next month.
4 Brian will meet his friends on Tuesday.
5 Michael will pass the math test.
6 I will join the tennis club.
7 We will eat Chinese food at 1:00 p.m.

C

1 1) He will see a doctor.
   2) He will go to bed early.
2 1) He will make a sandwich.
   2) He will order pizza.

WRAP UP

pp. 56~58

A

1 It was at Hyejin's house.
2 Mina and John came to the party.
3 She got a cap and a T-shirt (for her birthday).
4 She put her presents on the sofa.

B

1 will be a cook, He will make[cook] delicious food.
2 will be a singer, She will sing beautiful songs.
3 will be a teacher, He will teach English.

C

1 Tony and I were close friends.
2 I will learn taekwondo next month.
3 Ted bought his mother some flowers.
4 Anne will be late for school.
5 My sister broke my cell phone yesterday.
6 My family will travel to Busan this weekend.

7 My grandfather built our house 50 years ago.

8 Mike will fix my computer tomorrow.

D

1 1) She went to the beautiful beach.

  2) She ate a lot of seafood there.

2 1) I will be busy this Saturday.

  2) We will play basketball at[in] the park.

E

1 You will go to the horse farm.

2 You will ride a horse there.

3 You will go to Suwolbong Peak.

4 You will watch the sunset there.

F

1 woke up late this morning

2 He ran fast.

3 he missed the school bus

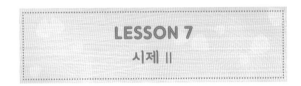

LESSON 7
시제 II

UNIT 1

pp. 60~61

A

1 We are staying in London.

2 Minhye is standing in line.

3 I am chatting online with my friend.

4 The boys are playing baseball.

5 My brother is using my smartphone.

6 They are swimming in the pool.

7 Joe and Karen are eating sandwiches in the kitchen.

8 Jenny is updating her blog.

B

1 is building a sand castle

2 is lying on the towel

3 is eating ice cream

4 are playing volleyball

C

1 1) I am studying for a math test.

  2) I am exercising at the gym.

2 1) I am baking a birthday cake.

  2) What are you doing?

  3) I am writing an essay.

UNIT 2

pp. 62~63

A

1 Amy was listening to music in her room.

2 Minsik and I were dancing on the stage.

3 I was waiting for Seungho.

4 They were having a birthday party.

5 My parents were climbing a mountain.

6 I was fixing my computer.

7 Jina was washing dishes in the kitchen.

8 David and Sue were taking a walk.

B

1 Luke was writing an email.

2 I was looking for my English book.

3 She was wearing sunglasses.

4 Joe and I were kicking a ball.

5 My father was reading a newspaper.

6 We were cleaning the classroom.

7 My mother was baking cookies.

C

1 1) was playing the violin at 10:00 a.m

  2) He was cleaning his room at 3:00 p.m.

2 1) was playing with her cat at 10:00 a.m

  2) She was watching a baseball game at 3:00 p.m.

WRAP UP

pp. 64~66

A

1 am using the computer

2 are driving too fast

3 are waiting for you

B

1 They[Kara and Jay] were moving a desk.

2 Bob was blowing up a balloon.

3 She[Tiffany] was writing ("celebrate") on the whiteboard.

C

1 I am studying French now.

2 The baby was smiling.

3 Ann is talking with her mother.

4 Carter and Jason were playing badminton.

5 Terry is singing a song in his room.

6 Sophie was wearing a cap.

7 My brother is painting the wall.

8 He was eating[having] lunch at the cafeteria.

D

1 1) My father is cleaning the living room.

   2) My brother is playing computer games in his room.

2 1) Jill was sleeping at home.

   2) Amy was studying in the library.

E

1 1) A monkey was eating a banana.

2 1) A bear was swimming.

   2) A giraffe was eating leaves (from a tree).

F

1 are eating sandwiches under a tree

2 is riding a bike

3 is reading a book on the bench

LESSON 8
조동사

UNIT 1
pp. 68~69

A

1 I can buy the backpack.

2 My uncle can fix the computer.

3 James and Suman can ride horses.

4 Hyunji can cook Italian food.

5 They can attend the meeting.

6 I can carry this heavy box alone.

7 We can read a book in English.

8 Sally and Jack can write in Chinese.

9 Jinsu can sing pop songs.

B

1 Sarah is able to play tennis.

2 Jongmin is able to play the violin.

3 Amy and Insu are able to ride a bike.

UNIT 2
pp. 69~70

A

1 You may use student discounts.

2 You may call me Joe.

3 Kate may borrow my textbook.

4 You may sit next to me.

5 You may play computer games for thirty minutes.

6 You may play the piano in the room.

B

1 You may bring your pet.

2 You may cross the street.

3 You may ride the rides.

UNIT 3
pp. 70~71

A

1 We should save energy.

2 I should finish the work today.

3 You should drink a lot of water.

4 We should tell the truth.

5 You should fasten your seat belt.

B

1 1) She should take[bring] a map.

   2) She should wear a helmet.

2 1) He should wear his hiking boots.

   2) He should take[bring] some water.

WRAP UP
pp. 72~74

A

1 Tarzan can talk with animals.

2 Po can do kung fu.

3 Spiderman can climb walls.

B

1 You should turn off your cell phone

2 You should not eat any food during classes.

3 You should bring your textbook for classes.

4 You should not chat with your classmates during classes.

C

1 They can[are able to] run fast.

2 You may[can] go to Sam's birthday party tonight.

3 You should drive slowly.

4 I can[am able to] play the flute.

5 You may[can] turn on the heater.

6 You should exercise every day.

7 She can[is able to] solve the math problem.

8 You may[can] borrow my game CD.

D

1 1) You may[can] use your dictionary.

   2) you may[can] go home

2 1) You should bring an umbrella.

   2) You should take the subway.

E

1 1) You should not touch pictures.
   2) take photos

2 1) You should wear a swimming cap.
   2) You should not run in the pool area.
   3) You may have[bring] a tube.

F

1 You should visit Seoul Tower. You can enjoy a great view.

2 You should visit Dongdaemun market. You can buy cheap clothes.

LESSON 9
to부정사와 동명사

UNIT 1
pp. 76~77

A

1 Sam decided to learn taekwondo.
2 My job is to fix a computer.
3 To talk with friends is fun.
4 My plan is to finish the work today.
5 To wake up early is not easy.
6 Taemin likes to listen to rock music.
7 Her wish is to buy a beautiful house.
8 I hope to meet my favorite singer.

B

1 My dream is to study fashion in Paris.
2 I want to buy a new bike.
3 To meet new people is fun.
4 Katie hopes to join the movie club.
5 Jay's goal is to be a good golfer.

UNIT 2
pp. 77~78

A

1 Playing soccer is fun.
2 Dan's goal is winning the gold medal.
3 I like surfing the Internet.
4 My hobby is taking pictures.
5 Keeping a pet is not easy.
6 Anne didn't go shopping yesterday.

B

1 Jerry enjoyed watching sitcoms.
2 His dream is being an astronaut.

3 Driving fast is dangerous.
4 My mother likes drinking coffee.

UNIT 3
pp. 78~79

A

1 I plan to go to Spain this winter.
2 You need to buy a new wallet.
3 Tom finished fixing his phone.
4 Eva promised to bring her camera tomorrow.
5 She avoided drinking Coke.
6 I decided to learn Chinese.
7 David practiced throwing the ball.

B

1 1) enjoys baking bread and cookies
   2) She wants to be a baker.
2 1) enjoys designing clothes
   2) He wants to be a fashion designer.

WRAP UP
pp. 80~82

A

1 I decided to go to New Zealand.
2 I need to buy a plane ticket.
3 I want to climb mountains.

B

1 Jongsu enjoys making model planes.
2 Jay plans to stay in Rome for a day.
3 Yongmin hopes to play soccer in the Premier League.

C

1 Being[To be] a writer is my dream.
2 Brian enjoys watching action movies.
3 Her job is teaching[to teach] Japanese.
4 John wants to help poor people.
5 I plan to visit my cousin this weekend.
6 Patrick finished solving the puzzle.
7 My homework is writing[to write] a book report.

D

1 1) His goal is winning[to win] first prize.
   2) He practices playing the piano every day.
2 1) She stopped eating fast food.
   2) She started doing[to do] exercise.

E

1 1) I want to join the hip hop dance club.

2) I enjoy dancing.

3) I wish to learn hip hop dance.

2 1) I want to join the rock band.

2) I enjoy playing the guitar.

3) I wish to play the electric guitar well.

F

1 My plan is to visit Australia this summer. I want to see kangaroos.

2 My plan is to visit Switzerland this summer. I want to eat fondue.

LESSON 10
대명사 it

UNIT 1
pp. 84~85

A

1 It is four twenty.

2 It is Wednesday.

3 It is August 14th.

4 It is cloudy.

5 It is 500 meters.

6 It is summer.

7 It is dark.

8 It rained a lot.

9 It is September 1st.

B

1 It is nine thirty in the morning.

2 It is fall in Korea.

3 It is October 15th today.

4 It was Sunday yesterday.

5 It will snow this weekend.

6 It is bright here.

7 It is New Year's Day.

C

1 1) It is July 24th.

2) It is five o'clock in the afternoon.

3) It is hot and sunny.

2 1) It is July 25th.

2) It is seven o'clock in the morning.

3) It is cold and windy.

UNIT 2
pp. 86~87

A

1 It is bad to tell lies.

2 It is fun to talk with friends.

3 It is interesting to read comic books.

4 It is necessary to keep your room clean.

5 It is important to be honest.

6 It was impossible to solve this problem.

7 It was hard to find your house.

8 It is great to use this machine.

B

1 It is hard to get up early.

2 It is interesting to read blogs.

3 It is important to have a dream.

4 It is good to write in a diary every day.

5 It was lucky to get the ticket.

6 It is safe to wear a helmet.

7 It is exciting to open a present.

C

1 1) It is healthy to drink a lot of water.

2) It is unhealthy to drink a lot of Coke.

2 1) It is healthy to eat vegetables and fruit.

2) It is unhealthy to eat fast food.

WRAP UP
pp. 88~90

A

1 It is December 25th.

2 It is Saturday. / It is Christmas Day.

3 It is eight o'clock.

4 It is snowing[snowy].

5 It is dark.

B

1 It is fun to drink juice with it.

2 It is easy to clean the floor with it.

3 It is possible to protect your fingers with it.

C

1 It is cloudy and windy today.

2 It is fun to take a picture.

3 It is May 5th tomorrow.

4 It is dangerous to travel alone.

5 It is winter in Australia.

6 It is important to keep promises.

7 It is 500 meters from here to the library.

8 It is hard to change a habit.

D

1 1) It was dark.

　2) It was scary to walk alone.

2 1) It was fun to ride the rides.

　2) it began to rain[raining]

E

1 1) It was December 23rd.

　2) It was snowy.

　3) It was fun to have a snowball fight.

2 1) It was July 12th.

　2) It was rainy.

　3) It was boring to stay at home.

F

1 It is cold outside. It is necessary to wear a thick coat.

2 It is rainy outside. It is necessary to carry an umbrella.

LESSON 11
형용사와 부사

UNIT 1
pp. 92~93

A

1 I bought a new smartphone.

2 The horror movie was scary.

3 I found the test difficult.

4 We stayed in a small hotel.

5 These boxes are heavy.

6 This scarf will keep you warm.

7 He told me an interesting story.

8 The news made him happy.

9 My brother is popular at school.

B

1 I bought fresh tomatoes.

2 The math test was easy.

3 The movie made me sad.

4 This onion soup is sweet.

5 They live in a big house.

6 Good food keeps you healthy.

7 Seven is a lucky number.

C

1 1) He was fat.

　2) He wore a blue jacket and white pants.

2 1) She was tall.

　2) She wore a white blouse and black skirt.

UNIT 2
pp. 94~95

A

1 The dog barks too loudly.

2 My brother is very tall.

3 Sadly, we lost the game.

4 Tom studied math really hard.

5 It rained heavily this morning.

6 Luckily, I found my cell phone.

7 The birds fly high in the sky.

8 The fruit was really fresh.

B

1 My father came home early.

2 Suddenly, the girl shouted. / The girl shouted suddenly.

3 The cake was really sweet.

4 I found the store[shop] easily.

5 Honestly, I lost your notebook.

6 I was very tired yesterday.

7 Dave entered the classroom quietly.

C

1 1) I shook badly.

　2) Sadly, I failed the audition.

2 1) I ran fast.

　2) Surprisingly, I won the race.

WRAP UP
pp. 96~98

A

1 They were very hungry.

2 It was very delicious.

3 They were very scared.

B

1 She is a careful driver. She drives a car carefully.

2 He is a fast runner. He runs fast.

3 She is a good violinist. She plays the violin well.

4 He is a hard worker. He works hard.

C

1 We should keep the street clean.

2 She talked quietly in the library.

3 This wallet is cheap and black.

4 John solved the math problem quickly.

5 I saw a famous singer at the restaurant.

6 Reading[To read] a book makes me sleepy.

7 Sadly, Joan will move to Seoul next month.

D

1 1) He was studying hard in his room.

   2) Suddenly, his cell phone rang. / His cell phone rang suddenly.

2 1) The road was very slippery.

   2) I walked very carefully.

E

1 1) Pink Shoes has many nice shoes.

   2) They are very comfortable.

   3) Pink Shoes will make you stylish.

2 1) Brown's Cakes has many pretty cakes.

   2) They are very delicious.

   3) Brown's Cakes will make your day special.

F

1 is carrying a heavy bag

2 is talking loudly on the phone

3 is holding beautiful flowers

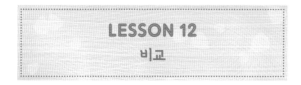

LESSON 12
비교

UNIT 1
pp. 100~101

A

1 This week is warmer than last week.

2 Ron studied harder than Anne.

3 Mina likes rice more than bread.

4 Joan is taller than her mother.

5 My brother's room is bigger than mine.

6 Health is more important than money.

7 This wallet is cheaper than that one.

8 Silk is softer than cotton.

9 Lucy's dog wakes up earlier than Lucy.

B

1 The Eiffel Tower is taller than the 63 Building.

2 The KTX is faster than the bus.

3 A watermelon is heavier than an orange.

C

1 1) likes emails more than letters

   2) Emails are faster than letters.

2 1) likes air conditioners more than fans

2) Air conditioners are cooler than fans.

UNIT 2
pp. 102~103

A

1 This is the most expensive car in this shop.

2 Jejudo is the largest island in Korea.

3 Today is the hottest day in August.

4 It is the most difficult chapter in this book.

5 Justin is the most popular boy in my class.

6 Juyoung is the fastest runner of the three.

7 The Louvre is the biggest museum in the world.

B

1 Seoul is the biggest city in Korea.

2 This church is the oldest building in this town.

3 The panda is the most popular animal in this zoo.

4 Tuesday is the busiest day of the week.

5 This toy is the cheapest of all.

6 Tom is the most diligent student in our class.

7 Mark is the richest man in our country.

C

1 1) is the lightest runner of the three

   2) He is the tallest runner of the three.

2 1) is the heaviest runner of the three

   2) He is the slowest runner of the three.

WRAP UP
pp. 104~106

A

1 1) The smartphone is lighter than the tablet PC.

   2) The tablet PC is heavier than the smartphone.

2 1) The smartphone is cheaper than the tablet PC.

   2) The tablet PC is more expensive than the smartphone.

B

1 Mt. Everest is the highest mountain in the world.

2 The Nile River is the longest river in the world.

3 The Pacific Ocean is the widest ocean in the world.

4 The cheetah is the fastest animal in the world.

C

1 Diamonds are harder than iron.

2 Russia is the largest[biggest] country in the world.

3 My boyfriend is more handsome than Brad.
4 The Incheon Bridge is the longest bridge in Korea.
5 Jay swims faster than Grace.
6 This camera is the most expensive of the four.
7 My computer is older than yours.

D

1 1) The rabbit ran faster than the turtle.
  2) the turtle crossed the finish line earlier than the rabbit
2 1) Prague was the most beautiful city of the three.
  2) Rome was the hottest city of the three.

E

1 1) Cox's Bazar Beach is longer than Ninety Mile Beach.
  2) Cox's Bazar Beach is the longest beach in the world.
2 1) Lake Baikal is deeper than Lake Tanganyika.
  2) Lake Baikal is the deepest lake in the world.

F

1 Online shops are more convenient than offline shops.
2 Online shops have more reviews than offline shops.
  [추가 답안] Online shops are cheaper than offline shops.
  [추가 답안] Online shops have longer shopping hours than offline shops.

Useful Patterns for Writing 1

1 My favorite color is blue.
2 Alex hates tennis.
3 Kate's favorite food is pizza.
4 My brother hates hot milk.
5 Anne's favorite city is Rome.
6 He hates math.
7 Nick's favorite subject is English.
8 Emma hates horror movies.
9 Her favorite month is April.
10 I hate Monday mornings.

Useful Patterns for Writing 2

1 Luke keeps his room clean.
2 John is tired of his old car.
3 My sister keeps the window open.
4 My grandmother is tired of this cold weather.
5 They keep the plan secret.
6 I am tired of my black hair.
7 Large[Big] windows keep the house bright.
8 Adam is tired of the work.
9 Emily keeps her nails short.
10 Carrie is tired of the busy city life.

Useful Patterns for Writing 3

1 Julie doesn't like Italian food.
2 I enjoy watching TV.
3 Sophia doesn't like chicken.
4 My father enjoys cooking.
5 I don't like her new book.
6 My friends enjoy playing baseball.
7 Henry doesn't like rock music.
8 We enjoy eating ice cream.
9 Terry doesn't like soccer.
10 My family enjoys traveling by train.

Useful Patterns for Writing 4

1 What[How] about studying together?
2 How long is your summer vacation?
3 What[How] about buying this watch?
4 How much do you love me?
5 What[How] about eating out tomorrow?
6 How often does Amy play the piano?
7 What[How] about watching the Olympic games on TV?
8 How much do you know about wine?
9 What[How] about going home now?
10 How long is the Great Wall of China?

Useful Patterns for Writing 5

1 I am sorry but I am busy now.
2 Thank you for calling me.
3 I am sorry but I don't know him.
4 Thank you for waiting for me.
5 I am sorry but I don't believe you.
6 Thank you for visiting our store[shop].
7 I am sorry but I hate pizza.
8 Thank you for inviting me.
9 I am sorry but I don't agree with you.
10 Thank you for sending me the present[gift].

Useful Patterns for Writing 6

1 Why don't you buy a laptop?
2 Would you help me?
3 Why don't you ask her?
4 Would you buy me a sandwich?
5 Why don't you take a bus?
6 Would you lend me your pen?
7 Why don't you eat dinner now?
8 Would you tell me your phone number?
9 Why don't you go to an ice rink with me?
10 Would you explain Korean culture?

Useful Patterns for Writing 7

1 My family came to see a new house.
2 The test proved to be difficult.
3 Carter came to give me a gift[present].
4 The man proved to be Jay's uncle.
5 Grace came to do homework with me.
6 The news proved to be true.
7 We came to visit Ron's house.
8 The thief proved to be Eric.
9 Emily came to say goodbye.
10 His concert proved to be successful.

Useful Patterns for Writing 8

1 I am afraid I can't answer the questions.
2 I am busy preparing for the English test.
3 I am afraid I can't remember your name.
4 Linda is busy practicing the piano.
5 I am afraid I can't fix your car.
6 She is busy cleaning her house.
7 I am afraid I can't meet you tomorrow.
8 James is busy playing computer games.
9 I am afraid I can't remember the password.
10 They are busy studying math.

Useful Patterns for Writing 9

1 Eva feels like going shopping today.
2 Do you mind bringing your camera?
3 I feel like going out now.
4 Do you mind taking a picture of me?
5 Ben feels like eating[having] a sandwich.
6 Do you mind taking off your hat?
7 Justin feels like reading this book.
8 Do you mind opening the door?
9 I feel like dancing with you.
10 Do you mind turning off the heater?

Useful Patterns for Writing 10

1 It is worth learning English.
2 Karen hopes to live in France.
3 It is worth watching the movie.
4 We hope to see you soon.
5 It is worth eating[having] dinner at[in] the restaurant.
6 I hope to find my dog.
7 It is worth listening to parents' advice.
8 Betty hopes to go to the Maroon 5 concert.
9 It is worth teaching children.
10 Dana hopes to be an actress.

Useful Patterns for Writing 11

1   Kelly is good at singing.
2   Erica is sad to leave this country.
3   Tony was pretty good at writing.
4   I am happy to hear the news.
5   She is pretty good at speaking Japanese.
6   Joe was glad to stay at the hotel.
7   My father is good at fishing.
8   Carol is sad to lose her cell phone.
9   I am good at drawing pictures.
10 We are happy to have a vacation.

Useful Patterns for Writing 12

1   Julia prefers spring to summer.
2   It is getting darker and darker.
3   I prefer blue to red.
4   This tree grows taller and taller.
5   My sister prefers orange juice to tomato juice.
6   My life is getting better and better.
7   Andrew prefers hip hop to rock music.
8   The Internet is getting faster and faster.
9   Young people prefer tennis to golf.
10 The weather[It] is getting colder and colder.